Fig. I

PARADIGM FOR CHANGE

Fig. I

PARADIGM FOR CHANGE

Community Social Work:
A Paradigm for Change

G. Smale, G. Tuson, M. Cooper,
M. Wardle and D. Crosbie

Published 1988
by the National Institute for Social Work
5 Tavistock Place, London WC1

ISBN 0902789 51 1

Printed by Waddington & Sons (Printers) Ltd., Fielden Square, Todmorden,
Lancs. OL14 7LE

Preface

This book is one of the outcomes of a Community Social Work Working Party set up in 1983 to "identify the core characteristics of community social work and its training implications." The working party became a major strand of the National Institute for Social Work's Practice and Development Exchange activities (PADE). PADE was established to provide information about innovations in the field of social care, to promote development work and the diffusion of new methods of practice.

When the working party was formed, one of the first major issues identified concerned the change from orthodox to community social work. The discussions which took place in the working party and in many subsequent contexts kept producing questions which could be summarised as follows:—

> "Community social work of the kind described by Barclay, has, typically, been developed in small units, often specially resourced and usually different from the rest of the department. Being innovatory projects they have usually grown organically rather than being planned from the start. How then can these approaches to practice be translated from 'project' work to mainstream agency work?"

This book addresses the practice dimension of this change which, characteristically, is incremental, evolutionary.

Root and branch re-organisations, typical of much service planning, may be likened to an ape walking through the jungle while his mind decides to evolve into a man. The risks of such rapid transformation could be considerable. Yet many creatures achieve a metamorphosis during their lifetime, achieving changes of the order of caterpillar to butterfly. These changes are organic and orderly, and follow the form of previous existence, maintaining all that is needed of the old whilst radically changing into the new. Buildings can be changed through planned demolition and reconstruction. Social services departments are open human organisations and change, particularly planned change, must be undertaken with a full awareness of what this means.

Throughout the writing of this book we have struggled with this central dilemma. We have stressed that community social work is an activity which evolves through partnerships between paid social work staff and other people in the community, including a variety of citizens, other agency staff and professionals. It follows that it is impossible to prescribe the detailed aims, methods and approaches of community social work from the outside of the social context, or community, that workers inhabit. However, we can draw on the experience of those who have made the journey, to describe the processes workers go through to arrive at aims and methods relevant to their practice. To achieve this our writing is of two kinds. Sometimes we are describing these processes; at other times, we are giving illustrations of practice reached by taking such a path.

A metaphor for describing this distinction is the music of Moussorgski's "Pictures at an Exhibition". This music has a major theme: the promenade. Other pieces of music are written to describe each picture as the composer walks round the gallery. The promenade links each picture and, inevitably, influences the pictures seen. In this book, the promenade is our description of a paradigm for change. This we offer as a path which can be followed and one which should lead to community social work. We depart from this path to illustrate what may be discovered, by presenting pictures drawn from our experience. We do not suggest these pictures will be the same for you. Readers will have to draw their own pictures with their own material.

The aim of this book is to contribute to the exchange of experience amongst practitioners and managers engaged in developing community social work. Ideas are presented for a practice theory based on our analysis of the practice of members of the working party and others engaged in the Community Social Work Exchange. The book is not drawn from a review of the available literature. Some references are included for people

4

to follow up other authors on specific issues, but many we have omitted, to maintain the directness of our discussion. We are aware of the need to write another book which discusses more fully some of the major theoretical issues raised here and relates these ideas to current research and practice literature.

The process of writing this book has varied, but is consistent with the enterprise that we are attempting to describe. Discussions around the themes of community social work took place within the working party. These were based on people's accounts of their practice experience and papers either specially written or previously prepared for some other context. The assumptions and thinking of that person were then teased out and exchanged with the thinking of others in the group. Notes, some of which were responding papers, were written incorporating many of the points raised in the discussions. Other responses or papers were written, and exchanged. The main themes relating to the change toward community social work have been drawn together and written up, absorbing parts of these discussions.

These social processes can be 'punctuated' in several ways. The conventional way is for the person holding the pen at the final stage, before submitting the book to press, to put his or her name on the book produced. This is in one sense fair, since they have literally 'written' the work. Yet in another sense, it completely masks the interactions that have taken place and the important fact that these ideas, and even more the practices they describe, are interpersonal events, the product of many people and more than any of these individuals could have produced on their own. To believe that individual talent alone somehow produces books would flatly contradict the view of social relations, social problems and so-called individual pathology taken in this book.

This is no superficial corporate or individual act of humility in acknowledging sources and influences, nor is it a way of thanking those who helped. It is a statement about the essentially interpersonal nature of social events, such as producing books. It is necessary to spell it out, for it is a central part of the substance of this publication.

To 'punctuate' any stream of ideas as being of one person is simple and normal. Individuals should be acknowledged according to this normality, for that is the world we live and make our living in. To 'punctuate' it only in this way is to do profound violence to the conceptualisations we are struggling with.

When you read these words that one of us has put down and others have produced through their talk and typing, can we really in any meaningful sense say that they are *our* ideas? Is the idea not now in your head, so is it not yours at this moment? Is it not now part of *your mind* rather than being a product of one, which is also what it is?

To have each paper individually acknowledged would be orthodox and, it could be said, an individual casework approach. To have them corporately labelled would be conveniently unorthodox and, possibly, a community work approach. To refuse to be seduced by this illusion of alternatives and to acknowledge the relationships between the individual and others and the corporate is another way of looking at it and is a community social work way of doing things.

Members of the Community Social Work Working Party who have participated throughout its existence are Bill Bennett, Mike Cooper, David Crosbie, Giles Darvill, Barbara Hearn, Gerry Smale, Brian Thomson, Graham Tuson, Mike Wardle. The following also participated and contributed for part of the time: Wendy Beecher, Peter Beresford, Vic Blickem, Lynette Domoney, David Gilroy, Tim Huntingford, Ela O'Farrell, Brian Parrott, Roy Pearson.

Those taking the conventional responsibility for the book are the authors named on the title page. Practice and Development Exchange was made possible by a generous grant from the Joseph Rowntree Memorial Trust, and we are particularly grateful to Robin Guthrie for his ideas and support. The Community Social Work Exchange is currently supported by the DHSS, the Scottish Office, and by the many agencies who enable their staff to participate.

We have been greatly helped with editorial comments from Daphne Statham and Margaret Hogan. Finally, this book would not have been possible without the tolerance, in the face of severe provocation, and the enduring skill of Betty Bennett.

Authors

Gerald Smale: Director of Practice and Development Exchange, National Institute for Social Work.

Graham Tuson: Lecturer in Social Work, University of Southampton.

Michael Cooper: Assistant Director, Wakefield Social Services Department.

Michael Wardle: Assistant Area Director, Newcastle upon Tyne Social Services Department.

David Crosbie: Research Fellow, National Institute for Social Work.

CONTENTS

PART I

From Here to Community Social Work

"There are no destinations, only journeys"

Chapter 1

Introduction: Points of Departure

A guide through the processes involved in making the transition from conventional social work to community social work practice needs to be akin to a music score. A music score provides a way of setting out the rudiments of a piece of music where the activities of a hundred or more people are co-ordinated, so all play their parts as the music unfolds through time. The music is nearly always recognisable as the same piece, but speed, tone, interpretation, even instrumentation may vary according to the idiosyncrasies of the people present on the day. Community social work is a whole approach, or set of attitudes, rather than a particular activity or series of activities. For this reason a neat description of community social work is not enough. Describing a symphony only goes a small way to telling you what it sounds like. In social work terms, a description of a specific set of methods or practices is like describing the part played by individual instruments.

We see community social work as the *mind* of the enterprise; a set of key connecting principles and strategies for organised social care and social work practice. We hope that this perception will become clearer as we articulate our assumptions. We will also tackle the problem of *defining* community social work and attempting to spell out the main building blocks of a practice theory to underpin thinking and action.

We present a *paradigm* for change. A paradigm is a 'pattern', an 'exemplar', an 'example'; it is a means to *discover* community social work. It is not a 'plan', a 'blueprint' or 'map' to be followed by others. The activities suggested by the paradigm will have to be moulded and changed to fit the circumstances of those attempting to use it. The paradigm is a *guide* to map making, to the processes the team may engage in to identify what it should do and how it can do it.

The Paradigm (see Fig. I, front endpaper)

The paradigm is a spiral, representing continuous, recurring activities that overlap, and so mirroring the cyclical nature of the developmental process. People engage in recurring activities but move on in developmental terms, as well as in time.

The diagram signposts the basic components required for a team to change orientation and extend their activities. The team, or members of it, will not proceed slavishly from one step to another. They might cross the circles and/or by-pass a group of activities or even do all these things at once and in parallel. Indeed it is probably impossible not to do this in practice, so we need to make explicit how the open system of the team and its activities are constantly being influenced by people outside the team. (This we illustrate in Chapter Seven.)

The planning and action involved in these changes are not 'armchair' topics for a 'team meeting'. Each set of activities involves work with people outside the team: the team will need to identify the themes which hold their practice together. The purpose of the paradigm is to help the team identify their goals and develop a clear and flexible strategy for achieving them. Without action and strategy, the changes the team wants to make may well be submerged in endless discussion on 'first aid' work.

We will briefly describe the paradigm; and the major points which correspond to subsequent chapters in the book. The first step in the paradigm is IDENTIFYING BASIC ASSUMPTIONS AND VALUES. The members of the team need to engage in continuous dialogue with a range of people outside and inside the team. The values of the organisation of which it is a part cannot be ignored nor those of its ultimate employers who may prescribe essential components of this value base. In addition, the team will need to take account of the value bases of the various professional* or occupational groups to which members belong. This is discussed in detail in Chapter 2.

The next stage in the paradigm, IDENTIFYING ACTIVITY AREAS, refers to the need for the team to recognise its own pattern of existing relationships with people in the community, in other agencies, within workers' own agencies and with the new activities it wishes to generate. These are the processes that team members need to be aware of and engage in. We emphasise process because workers are part of, and party to, these interactions, not outside, observing and doing things for them or to them as if they were objects. Chapter 3 sets out our picture of these characteristic activities and relationships. There we identify nine *key characteristics of community social work* drawn from our practice experience and presented as examples of the kind of processes in which teams will engage, together with examples of the more specific activities involved.

Chapter 4 proposes a framework for IDENTIFYING A TEAM DEFINITION OF COMMUNITY SOCIAL WORK. There are already many definitions of community social work, just as there are many ways of understanding and using the concept of community, but we believe it is necessary for a team of workers to have their own common understanding of what they mean by community social work and community. To present a definition of community social work at the beginning of the book might seem logical. But to do so would imply that social workers should first define community social work, then identify who they are going to work with and what methods they are to use.

Instead, by first analyzing their activities and engaging in new areas, the team will at the same time be formulating their own definition. Following the logic of this argument, we present our

* We use the term "professional" in the sense that some footballers are "professional," meaning that they are paid, that their training and skill make them fitter and more consistent than amateurs who can play football. This is, of course, not always true even of footballers! So, by this definition, a home help is as much a "professional" as a CQSW qualified social worker.

definition of community social work and a discussion of it at this particular juncture.

In Chapter 5 we underline the need to SET UP PROCEDURES FOR MONITORING PRACTICE and discuss the issues involved in developing the knowledge and skills of the team by COMPARING AND CONTRASTING CURRENT AND FUTURE PRACTICE. We also look at the modes of staff development relevant to developing NEW SKILL AREAS. Our view is that it is not enough just to train individual staff; the whole organisation needs to be constantly changing to meet the evolving tasks of the agency. Thus the next step in the paradigm is ORGANISATIONAL DEVELOPMENT NEEDS, discussed in Chapter 6.

We are assuming that by this stage the team will have extended their range and understanding of the partnerships they have entered into. Feedback from these activities and attempts to start new practice will supply essential evidence for discussions of 'skills' or 'organisation development' needs. We have stressed that 'planning' is through action not hypothetical discussion, and so propose a pragmatic 'suck it and see' approach to development, not change through grand design. In the experience of practitioners who have made such transitions, the time-scale is measured in years, not months.

By this stage the team's own map of their current and future work should become clearer. In Chapter 7 we look at how a team sets about DEVELOPING CHANGE PLANS, and attempt to provide some clues about the planning process as an aid to identifying and keeping in mind overall strategies. This touches on technical planning issues, and supplements but does not substitute for other publications on planning, for example Miller and Scott (1984); Hedley (1985). Such publications will help managers/practitioners through these stages in the technology of setting up MONITORING PROCESSES.

Engaging in new activity areas

Finally, the diagram brings us round to RE-THINKING ASSUMPTIONS and then RE-DEFINING COMMUNITY SOCIAL WORK, and so in Part II of the book we review our own assumptions and offer ideas for a new practice theory. We do not think that values, aims and objectives should remain constant despite people's experiences. This is especially true when those experiences involve engaging with others both as 'a means' and as 'the end' of the team's endeavours. We stress that constant change in the team is endemic in the paradigm and in these activities.

The paradigm is based on the premise that different teams can and will start from different points; it does not prescribe specific goals, but focuses on the *process* teams will engage in, the continuous and recurring relationships they have with other parts of the organisation to which they belong, and with the communities within which they work. Others have developed the practice of community social work by identifying certain constituents such as 'localisation' (Bayley, Seyd and Tennent 1985; Bennett 1980; Cooper 1980; Hadley and McGrath, 1980) or by emphasising indirect service (Sinclair et al 1983), or local participation (Beresford and Croft 1986). We, however, have different starting points — namely our assumptions about change, innovation and the centrality of interpersonal relationships. These we set out in Chapter 2.

Chapter 2

Basic Assumptions About Community Social Work

Notes on values, attitudes, and the changes involved in community social work

Our belief is that community social work involves a way of thinking about people and problems that is fundamentally different from most orthodox social work thinking. Yet it is also the case that others doing community social work will not think in this way. This difference of opinion is not unique to community social work. For example to start from an assumption that the world is round rather than flat makes very little difference to day-to-day living. Columbus probably sailed his ship in exactly the same way as any other competent sea captain of the day. However, his different *vision* of the world made fundamental differences. He sailed to 'the edge of the world' and beyond. So the new thinking changes some things, but not others. Now the Vikings almost certainly went 'beyond the edge of the world', also without understanding the 'new way of thinking' about the world, just as many social workers have extended the range of their activities beyond casework, without changing their basic ideas about people or problems. In a limited sense, it is not necessary to have a different vision — you keep sailing west and hope for the best. Another vision of social work, 'community work', is also different but equally restricted if it excludes casework. A new theory will help us do things we have never been able to do before, without being afraid of falling off the edge of the world (or ignoring traditional 'clients').

We recognise that our subjective values are involved in presenting this paradigm, and we invite those using it to build in their own. To follow certain processes excludes certain outcomes; it is difficult to see how 'loving thy neighbour' could lead to the gas chambers. But though the paradigm is not neutral, neither is it a prescription of a definite set of values based on an analysis of what happens in communities, or to the people within them. It can perhaps be accurately described as 'agnostic'.

It is necessary for social workers to be explicit about their values. They need to evaluate critically the part their social conditioning, including their professional training, plays in forming their beliefs, attitudes and actions. The values and assumptions which influence practice need to be shared within the team and with those to whom social workers are, and should be accountable. Social workers cannot avoid their own beliefs about how people should relate to each other and they must be clear and open on major issues. For example we believe we should confront racism and sexism. We also believe we should confront the stigmatisation of people as clients.

Central to this change is a shift in our thinking from focusing on identified clients to the relationships *between* people; from thinking about groups or 'classes' of people to thinking about the relationships between people across groups, classes and organisations. This shift in thinking from the parties in relationship to *patterns of relationship* is deceptively easy to say, yet often extremely difficult to put into practice. In some ways it has also long been recognised. Most social or psychological theories attempt to understand people and their behaviour. They often analyse the influences on a person of other people and other factors in the environment. Yet it is typical that one or other party in these relationships is held to be constant as if *they* were not influenced by the other. The analysis tends to see influence as a one-way process, as if people can ever relate like that in real life. The difference suggested here is the difference between ecology and the science of individual organisms.

 For us, a social problem is no longer located in an individual person, or individual social unit such as a family, but in the patterns of relationship which define the social situation of that individual. Holder and Wardle give an extended practice example of what is involved in the shift of thinking required for community social work (Holder and Wardle 1981, Chapter 8):

The Edwards family had become framed as a 'multi-problem family'. They lived on a 'problem' street on a 'problem' estate. The problems *of* the family were framed by professionals and others in the family social environment as problems *in* the family. Everything would be all right for everybody if only the mother became more competent; the sons law-abiding; and the daughters sexually self-restrained. In short, their situation, and that of the neighbours, schools and social work agencies with whom the families were in relationship, was universally understood and responded to in terms of individual pathology and the pathology of the individual family. To focus on the family and its members in this way is legitimate for they are one side of the equation, but it is also to ignore the pattern of relationships which define the family as problematic in the first place.

Interventions made on the basis of such understandings had been going on for years and had helped create and perpetuate a culture of scape-goating within the family, and between the family and its wider social network. To say of someone that she is scape-goated is to say something about that individual and those who 'scape-goat'; it is a shorthand way of describing a set of *relationships,* and not something about the exclusive character or qualities of the individual. So to say the Edwards family became scape-goated is to use a loose metaphor to capture how they had become enmeshed in a binding web of blaming and blamable relationships. It was those relationships which became the focus of social work intervention and which are analysed and described by Holder and Wardle.

The range of interventions, and their relationships to one another were varied and complex. They involved opportunistic work with neighbours aimed at helping them shift their focus of blame from the Edwards to the wider context of the street and the estate; working with a tenants' group, and the relationships between the housing department and the residents, and between residents themselves. Several of these interventions occurred at the same time, rather than sequentially, and this is a significant feature of effective practice within complex patterns of relationship. For example, the Edwards' neighbour became angry with the social worker who had been clearing away rubbish from the Edwards' garden. The neighbour's expressed anger allowed the possibility of changing the relationship between the neighbour and the Edwards. By just removing the rubbish, the worker could have been acting *as if* all that needed to change was one party to the relationship between the Edwards and the neighbour, i.e. the Edwards. By engaging with the neighbour at the same time, the worker acknowledged that the problem was not the rubbish *per se,* but the attitudes, expectation and behaviour of the Edwards and those in relationship with them. The relationship had to be responded to as well as the rubbish, and the individuals who deposited the rubbish. (The theoretical ideas underlying this analysis are discussed further in Part II of this book.)

Community social work: practice or just preaching?

In the debates, arguments and analysis of our own community social work practice and observation of that of colleagues, we have identified the following further basic assumptions, which underpin the whole of the paradigm and our reasons for presenting our thinking and experience in this way.

A curious phenomenon seems constantly to develop in discussions of community social work. Often early in the discussion there is general agreement that the aims and objectives of social workers should be negotiated and planned in partnership with a variety of other people. Partnership is a key element in community social work. The identification of needs, resources, methods, priorities and a plan of action will all come through these reciprocal relationships. This is what is meant by the interweaving of formal and informal care. These partnerships with a range of people including other professionals, members of communities, 'informal carers', neighbourhood volunteers and organisations, and other resource providers, are an integral part of community social work. This partnership goes beyond consultation to shared decision making based on a recognition of who can offer what to the resolution of social problems. Accountability and responsibility for work also needs to be shared within these partnerships.

It would seem logical that the discussions amongst the social work staff about what they do should stop at a preliminary point, to be continued in partnership with a wider group of participants.

To go further in defining what needs to be done and how it should be accomplished would contradict this key part of community social work practice.

However, typically, social work staff and managers do go on to discuss and decide on a range of issues from 'organising patch teams', to organising responses to individual social problems, without entering into partnerships with a wider group of people or organisations outside the social work agency. Yet still all those involved may be committed to the belief that they work out aims and objectives through a review of needs and resources *with* a wide range of other people. They may even believe it so strongly that they think they are already doing it.

Relationships: planning by objectives or ways to plan?

We must then address the apparent contradiction between deciding aims through partnerships, and social workers and their managers planning their work in an ivory, or, should we say, plate-glass tower. We have been aware of it for several reasons, but it was particularly highlighted for us by the way we set out to plot the course of change from orthodox to community social work.

When we first began we thought it would be helpful to draw up a flow chart which describes the steps to be taken. This flow chart would be one way of looking at 'the process'. It would describe how a team or an agency could get from the status quo to community social work. This immediately presented several problems. People start from different places. A flow chart model identifies a linear process implying a final destination and it suggests a series of tasks, some of which are to be completed before others can begin. In short, the flow chart could have been seen as a critical path analysis. Our discussions on the nature of community social work, however, led us to see that such a model was, at best, inadequate and, at worst, dangerously misleading.

The assumption of partnership with others means that there can be no internally generated fixed destination; that community social work is essentially about the *processes* the workers engage in, the *relationships* they make and how they maintain and change them. These processes generate the specific aims and objectives of the workers and those they share work with. In the end these may be the same as those generated by either 'case-work' or 'community work', or through some other process, say social science research or the application of political theory. What is different about 'community social work' is that these aims and objectives are generated through different processes. In short, community social work cannot be identified by aims and objectives alone.

The apparent contradiction between 'working in partnership' and 'management decision making' can be resolved if we keep clear *who* should make decisions about *what* and in *what* form. We assume that the general goals and objectives of agencies will be laid down by central or local government, or articles of association. We suggest that social workers need to 'get their act together' about their contribution to the processes of social care. But, they should recognise that this is *a part,* and by no means all, of care in the community. *They can only clarify their contribution.* They are not in a position to prescribe the final shape of patterns of care that inevitably involve many other people's independent actions. Their contributions to these patterns can only happen through discussions, negotiations or consultations with other people. So it is with this book. It is not a prescription about objectives or methods of work, but a guide to how these ends could be identified and achieved. In our view, community social work is essentially about the *means* through which social workers contribute to social care. What we suggest is the range of processes that workers and managers need to engage in, and the questions that need to be addressed.

Our fundamental assumption, then, is that community social work is the process through which workers arrive at goals and objectives by working in partnership with others in their environment. It follows that a detailed prescription of com-munity social work goals and methods cannot be drawn up outside of the context of the work.

This approach does not eschew the importance of structure, objectives and plans; indeed, it is designed to help staff draw up their own, relevant to the circumstances within which they work and the people with whom they do it.

We stress that community social work involves the team in using methods of work which are relevant to the idiosyncrasies and history of the relationship between the needs and the resources of the human and material environment of which it is a part. It follows that the way social work is organised and what is actually done will vary from place to place, from community to community.

The following story illustrates the spiralling process of perpetual change through which a social work agency moved in identifying some interconnected needs at a general level, and engaged in partnership discussions as a consequence, which in turn altered some of the original goals and methods. It illustrates the way in which the social work agency contributes to a pattern of care by the processes in which it engages with others in the community, as against seeking to impose a prescribed structure of care.

An area officer was concerned about the general absence of inter-agency activity in his 'patch'. One day, as part of his practice of getting about and meeting people, he happened to join a conversation between the local vicar and the team's community liaison worker, in which the vicar was showing his concerns about a flat adjacent to his church which was empty and becoming dilapidated through lack of use. The area officer identified two possibilities. Firstly, from his own observations, and reports from residents to staff within his team, he was aware of the need for some form of 'drop-in' centre in the middle of town for use by elderly and retired people. Secondly, he was aware that the flat in question backed on to a large school room which was under-used. He thought that if it were possible to use the flat, it might then be possible to expand into the other building.

From such a beginning a process of partnership developed between the vicar; the trustees of the church buildings; local residents; the local probation service; the Manpower Services Commission; and other organisations; all of which contributed to forming and re-forming the aims and strategies originally developed within the area team. So, for example, the probation service, which had been seeking room in the local social services area office, used the flat as a location for some of the community service activities with a view to basing a reporting centre there, although in the end after discussion with other users, did not do so.

Community social work: a holistic view

We have stressed that a fundamental assumption we make is that *the way* in which social workers set about reviewing their practice is, in itself, a central dimension of community social work. It is about the relationship that workers engage in with others, and how their behaviour within relationships brings about change. An example may help to show why we think this is a fundamental assumption.

On one estate there were many referrals of elderly people and of adolescents and young children. A number of these people's problems were found to relate to a breakdown in the relationships between elderly people and the children on the estate. Further investigation revealed that the noise and boisterous activities of the children and adolescents was upsetting some elderly people who, in turn, complained about the noise, which provoked the youngsters to further antagonism. This precipitated requests for re-housing from the elderly people and the involvement of police and other agencies with the children. Petitions were raised, a youth club temporarily closed, and elected members involved.

When workers investigated this 'breakdown in relationships' further, they discovered that the children's playground was sited near the old people's flats, while the seats used by the latter were situated near the larger houses where young families lived. Whilst this in itself was only a contributory factor to the difficulties, it was important to include work with the housing and leisure and recreation departments to attempt to get the seats and playground switched over. This built on earlier work which had developed relationships with these departments. The intervention was part of a strategy that included work with individual elderly people, adolescents, families and networks of both local resident groups and other significant local agencies.

The significance of the examples lies in the portrayal of the importance of relationships *between* people, be they represented as individuals, or members of groups or classes. This emphasis on interpersonal relationships leads us to consider the intra and inter-team relationships as central to the practice of community social work.

Community social work and 'the team'

Readers will notice that we use the term 'team' throughout. This is deliberate. We argue that the smallest unit of staff which can engage in community social work is a team of workers. Individuals cannot be 'community social workers' on their own, since the variation and breadth of tasks goes well beyond the capacity of any one person. On the other hand, it has been demonstrated in practice that teams of workers can adopt a community social work approach even if, and often despite, the fact that the rest of their department works in a different way. Indeed, it follows from our assumptions that teams working in different environments are likely to adopt different approaches to community social work, as we have already stated. We do not use 'team' as synonymous with a group of fieldworkers. It may include other categories of workers such as residential, day care staff and home helps, or it may include members of other agencies, or be entirely composed of non-fieldwork staff.

There are examples around the country of teams consisting of inter-agency personnel. Indeed, it may be the case that such teams formed on the basis of some common interest are more likely to develop the relationships and practices characteristic of good team-work than are the conventional teams out of which the members operate. In Normanton, for example, a grouping of health visitors and area office staff developed out of a common need to monitor and manage 'packages' of community care for old people.

Early meetings developed into working relationships in the area, which removed the need for different agencies, or parts of the same agency, to refer cases for different inputs of services. Thus the approach to the use of residential care changed for all agencies along with changes in role distinctions between differently based carers. It also had the effect of encouraging welfare agencies to perceive more clearly the place of informal care systems in the community.

It is no accident that, whilst the imagination has been fired by the patch or localisation portrayal of community social work, the accounts by Bennett (1982), Cooper (1982), Honor Oak Team (1981), Holder and Wardle (1981) say as much, if not more, about teamwork (or some other shorthand word for team relationships), than about local offices, patch team structures, etc.

Sharing together as a team the individual philosophies and value systems of all team members is an essential ingredient of team working. We think that community social work can only be achieved from the basis of such co-operation. This means that a team's ways of working on relationships becomes significant. Reading about what others do and agreeing with it is one thing. Doing it is another. Since relationships are about what is *between* people, this implies that all parties are inescapably involved both actively and passively, activist and recipient. So relationships are not a phenomenon which a team can choose to develop or ignore — they exist and cannot be disregarded.

Such an approach necessitates changes in the development of staff and supervision skills. For example, a fundamental weakness of much supervision of fieldwork practice is the dependence on verbal or written reports of practice, and thus reliance on an ability to be wise after the event. Negligible attention is paid to the behaviour of the worker and the subsequent observable effects on others. The very structure of carrying out practice teaching and supervision away from the action makes this normal but it is not inevitable. It is predominantly absent from many day and residential care settings though advocates of family therapy have demonstrated, amongst other things, the value and efficacy of live supervision for practitioners and the people they work with (Smale 1987).

The transition from individualised working with individual clients, to teams working with individuals, groups and networks has some important inherent problems. In their research into practice in social services departments, Stevenson and Parsloe (1978) were critical of social workers' inability to work effectively in groups, not least of all their own staff groups. We might speculate that individualist and isolated ways of working, whilst ostensibly being members of a 'team', reflect and reinforce a

28

similar practice in the community. If practice in the community inextricably involves working with varieties of networks, individuals and groups, then the social worker's own team and agency must be considered and worked with similarly.

Rather than being considered an optional post-professional package therefore, team development and the promotion of team building is a constituent activity for all those practising community social work. The team becomes the focus for planning and for supervision. Promoting and maintaining team and inter-team relationships supports, stimulates and directs the efforts of team members in working with others in the networks of the local community. The development of shared leadership within the team fosters individual and collective vision and responsibility. It encourages the social worker to work in a similar way with others. Innovation and risk-taking by the social worker within a context of common concern, support and creativity in the team can offer more resources to communities than the lone individualist ever could. The team base is of crucial importance.

A way of life

Pursuing the importance of team relationships as a base for promoting work with social relationships in the wider context implies a different kind of life for those engaged in community social work. It straddles two different stereotypes of social work: one offering a technical, methodological focus, for example behaviour modification, and portraying social work in tight scientific terms (Sheldon 1980; Goldberg, Gibbons and Sinclair 1985); the other a pragmatic, descriptive account of how things actually work in experience, documenting anecdotal evidence which leaves the reader interested and even impressed (Currie and Parrott 1981; Hadley, Dale and Sills 1984). Neither helps workers make sense of all their work in their own local situation nor do they always help in choosing when a particular technique or method is appropriate.

Both approaches can contribute to helping describe what community social work is about. But for helping guide what to do, something else is required. Relationships, networks and team work offer a third dimension, which we refer to as a 'way of life'. This does not mean eating, sleeping and dreaming community social work twenty-four hours a day. It means social workers responding as genuine people and eschewing both professional helping roles and a detached bureaucratic stance.

Some social services have moved on from being totally pragmatic in responding to the most urgent pressing demands made of them, and adopted a rational technical approach to planning. In this they seek to define and assess need based on so-called objective criteria, typically hard figures about their clientele. There is a danger that this approach compounds the tendency of many departments to focus on what to do *to* or *for* 'clients', rather than to work *with* them and people in their networks. Community social work requires the whole process of needs assessment, service planning and the designing of service delivery to be a negotiated process.

What do we mean by plan? A drawing for a house is prepared by experts and when the house is built, it is an abstraction of a given reality. To plan such a house is essential for building it properly. But a 'home' cannot be created in this way. To plan a 'home' we think it important to develop a set of agreements which will influence a series of future behaviours. Perhaps 'contract' would be a better metaphor to use than 'plan'. We should remember that any marriage is a living example of the problems of such planning or contracting. In reality such arrangements evolve over time in unforeseen ways. Perhaps they can only be planned in retrospect!

This is not an attack on rational planning. It is a recognition that many people *are* part of the patterns of social care to which the department's activities contribute. It is only 'rational' to recognise the need for discussion with these people in 'planning' or 'contracting' services *with* them. It is only rational to recognise the shortcomings of this part of the process.

Innovation and change: the exception or the rule

Developing community social work requires workers to change their current practices. Change is often considered undesirable and disruptive. This is an understandable, but incomplete perception of the nature of 'change'. Experience teaches us, when we allow it, that life is not stable, but there is a human and necessary tendency in us which leads us to behave as though it were. To live by the belief that 'the only certainty is uncertainty' is an exhausting business. Pushed to its apparent logical conclusion it is also an unproductive creed, for we should then never plan anything. To deny that 'change' is the essence of life is, however, also unproductive, leading to sterile activity increasingly unrelated to the pressures and issues it is intended to deal with. Life *is* change, and the task of the change agent is to harness such activity and redirect it. Change is opportunity — its more extreme forms offer the crisis interventionists their basic modus operandi. Innovation *may* result from a set of carefully selected assumptions and plans; but more often it really depends on seemingly more opportunist, more free thinking, although skilful, approaches to getting things done differently.

Innovation often occurs when people are stuck. The solutions to problems they apply do not work, yet they continue to be applied for they are the only ones known. To unstick these situations requires ideas from outside the given assumptions people make. It is inherently difficult to plan your way to such innovation.

These dimensions are easily overlooked in practice, because it is extremely difficult to 'see' the relationships of which you are a part, act differently to change them, and still 'see' them as they change. Here perhaps is a clue as to why defining community social work is so difficult. Those who are good at doing 'it', changing relationships of which they are a part, cannot easily describe 'it' because they have never observed 'it' being done — they have simply done 'it'. What they have done is to manage being on the boundary — being on the margin. To manage this boundary task of seeing the relationships of which you are a part in order to change them requires considerable skill.

Such a view of change and its centrality to community social work will undoubtedly make more demands on practitioners. Despite pleas to the contrary, bureaucratised social work with its attendant 'blueprint' planning is not as uncomfortable as many believe. Instead of planning what to do after a systematic analysis of needs and resource and then ploughing on relentlessly to fulfil the plan, the practitioners must use the planning process to equip themselves to read and understand the situation in which they find themselves *as it happens*. They must be able to 'work on the run'.

Managers and practitioners involved in community social work will experience substantial and frequent change in all aspects of their practice and work life. They will visibly demonstrate their part in the processes. The approach is not easy, not without struggle and pain, and requires commitment of a high order.

The nature of the ever changing social work organisation

Organisational change is often tackled as if departments or agencies were machines. They are re-organised or re-designed on the drawing board of some office and then re-shaped in much the same way as a building might be adapted or a new design of car introduced. Organisations are not machines; they are more organic than mechanistic entities and have a maze of living links with people both outside and within them. These relationships become 'institutionalised' over time, in some cases as rules, or as norms and expectations that govern or guide behaviour. These become 'taken for granted'. Organisations seem to achieve a certain stability but, in fact, they never stay the same. Re-organising these entities is more like re-designing a garden than a building. It cannot be done without killing off living parts of the garden and the 'new shape' cannot be achieved without enabling and waiting for the required new parts to grow. Expectations people have of each other within an organisation also have to change. The passage of *time* is a crucial issue for living entities. What organisation chart gives any clue about the significance of time?

Moreover, the aims of social workers themselves are often about promoting change. This means that they take on a role similar to that of a gardener within their environment. Not in the sense that the gardener decides what lives and dies, and what grows where and how big it should be. The social worker's 'garden' is full of people, not plants, people who have their own ideas and often more real power than 'the gardener'. But a gardener in the sense that their job is to be part of developing or sustaining or inititiating parts of the whole, or to engage in changing relationships between the parts. It would be wise of social workers to recognise that they cannot cause 'growth' or 'change' any more than a gardener can *cause* plants to grow; they can only intervene to influence these processes.

Within a human environment this means the change agent has to join with different parts of the whole, that is, with different people and different organisations, but then withdraw and move on. The social worker may form or join a neighbourhood group or a family for a small part of its existence, to help promote certain ends, and then withdraw and move on. The partnerships the worker has should be continually changing. In a human organisation, these external fluctuating relationships will inevitably have repercussions within the organisation. It is for these reasons that we see change as an essential, normal and constant feature of social work organisations.

But the uncertainty of change causes stress (see e.g. Marris 1974). Recognising and reviewing the effects of change in the organisation and its tasks requires planning skills. Under these circumstances staff training, support, supervision and organisation development are crucial. This is why they have an essential place in the paradigm.

Management assumptions

Changes of attitudes cannot be prescribed nor, we believe, can they be 'taught' in any narrow sense of the word. They can, however, be fostered and nurtured by the use of certain managerial strategies or techniques consistent with the aims of the social work organisation.

If we assume that the aim of much social work intervention is to achieve the greater autonomy of people receiving services, then central to the successful management of community social work is the recognition that decision making should be participative; that it should work, as far as possible, by consensus; and that its goal should be that priorities are established as locally as possible to fit local circumstances. The concept of participation in this context requires recognition that 'management' includes those in receipt of service as well as those providing it, not just those traditionally seen as 'managers', such as team leaders and area directors.

The concern for participation and consensus is founded on the recognition that all people have a degree of power which they consciously or unconsciously, explicitly or implicitly, exercise. This power can be manifested through different forms of authority which are inherent in all situations where decisions have to be made and priorities established. It is useful to introduce here the three forms of authority identified by Payne and Scott (1982), namely, positional authority, sapiental authority and the authority of relevance.

'Traditional' management at its worst inevitably over-values positional authority at the expense of the other two forms and results in a centralised, directive style, restrictive of initiative on the part of those 'further down' the hierarchy and exclusive of the recipients of service. The aims of such authority are constantly sabotaged by those whose power is unrecognised and so unmobilised for a common goal. The energy and concern of such centralised activity then gets diverted from the task, to controlling members of the organisation. Innovation, instead of being prized as a potential way of bettering the organisation, becomes distrusted as a further symptom of deviance and as a threat to central control.

We are not advocating an abdication of positional authority in favour of a democracy constipated by perpetual consultation, but a much broader, more flexible view of power and authority. Our experience has shown this leads to sounder decisions, to priorities which hold because they are seen to be relevant and felt to be 'owned'.

The struggle to obtain consensus in management contributes to, and is informed by, these values. It is unlikely that all concerned on all issues at all times will come to a common mind. Explicit conflict is a feature of consensus management. However, if the process is participative, it is usually the case that decisions become acceptable because individual points of view have been weighed, even when they have not prevailed. Local priority setting is best achieved where the link between the decision-making process and resulting activity is manifest to all concerned and includes the views of as many as possible of those involved.

The relationship between the team and others

Teams need to look outward towards the community they are part of, focusing on their place in the patterns of needs, developments and resources within that community. They should not be inward-looking, focusing primarily on office and departmental bureaucracy and the needs which they generate. In short, they should not treat the community as an external object.

The team needs to promote 'transparent' care systems within the community of which it is a part: an open understanding of the processes involved in 'care' and their contribution to them. For example — what happens when a child or adult comes 'into care'; what kind of problems lead to that happening and who defines them as problems; where are decisions taken and by whom; what problems are solved by deciding that a person is 'suitable' for one form of care rather than another; what happens if they do not 'qualify'? This kind of openness between the professionals and others in the community develops awareness that the caring task is a shared responsibility. An understanding grows about what kinds of actions are appropriate to offer at which stage, and that if a limited offer is made, it is not necessary or expected that it becomes a lifetime's commitment — other courses of action are available as needs change. Otherwise what was apparently a short-term need evolves into a long-term task.

To put such an approach into practice the professional team needs to develop a collective body of knowledge about 'care in the community': what kind of networks exist in different parts of the neighbourhood, who are the key figures within them, who does what best? In short, it is necessary to understand the local 'cultures' of care. Work carried out by members of ethnic minorities with their own members has led the way in demonstrating how this culturally specific work can and should be done. There will be many cultures within any community: the social work team will need to be actively alive to such cultures, and work continually with them.

Chapter 3

Identifying and Engaging in Community Social Work: What to do and how to start doing it

Key characteristics

In this chapter we offer some answers to the questions, "What do people *do* when they do community social work?" "How do they set about doing it?" There are no simple answers. Here we draw from reflections on our own direct experience of developing community social work in different settings and from our observations of other social work teams engaged in the same processes.

We have identified nine major characteristics of community social work. They are to:—

1. engage with people in the community in setting aims and objectives;
2. engage in identifying community resources for care;
3. identify and review types and methods of intervention;
4. seek ways of sharing in the social problems of the community;
5. engage in negotiating 'boundaries' with other organisations;
6. engage in negotiating 'boundaries' between different parts of the organisation;
7. work out ways of sharing work in the team;
8. set up ways of recognising and recording work; and,
9. where appropriate, set up decentralised, locally autonomous management procedures for allocating task responsibilities.

These characteristics bear in mind the view that social work interventions are focused upon relationships between people rather than upon individuals or classes of individuals. They attempt to draw attention to crucial patterns of relationships among the people involved in care in the community. These process aims are not canonical and a particular team may develop others, athough we would be surprised if there were not significant similarities with our own.

They are not presented in priority order, nor as a progression; it is not necessary to have completed 1 before moving on to 2, and so on. All are 'community social work' and in any action all are happening simultaneously. It is paradoxical that effectively and efficiently managed work has to be planned and reviewed sequentially, yet *at the same time,* it is part of a cyclical process. This relationship between linear and circular action and analytical thought is inherent in the paradigm.

1. **To engage with people in the community in setting aims and objectives.**

This is, perhaps, the most global and the most intimidating of all the process aims. It is helpful to take a concrete example.

Let us assume that a need has been identified for a carers' support scheme in a neighbourhood by a team member working with elderly people. It would be possible to consult 'the community' by advertising and holding a public meeting; experience, however, suggests that if that is all that is done the response is likely to be poor. It is likely to be more profitable for team members to spend time identifying ways in which they are already in touch with members of the community to whom such a development would be most immediately relevant. These will probably include the domiciliary care service, meals on wheels, lunch clubs, casework service, possibly a list of those for whom telephones are provided, and so on. The process of pooling this information will generate other useful information. For example, who are the articulate members of this particular community of interest; who are the organisers? It is also likely to generate lateral thinking in the team — why only those caring for the elderly? What about unsupported mothers, parents of handi-

38

capped children, and so on?

Once specific people in the community have begun to be identified from existing known information, the process of engagement will happen at a number of levels — individual discussions; formal/semi-formal discussion at lunch clubs; chats between home helps and social workers. The team will also need to consult with people in other parts of the community who are also engaged in caring — health visitors, GPs, voluntary agencies. It is much more likely that people who have been involved at this level will respond to an invitation to attend a meeting about the proposed scheme than if the invitation arrives 'cold' through the letter box. The consultation also makes it possible for the social work team to plan an agenda for the meeting which reflects the concerns of those for whom the service is intended, rather than only the concerns of the social workers. Similarly, any such meeting can approach the shared task of debating the nature and goals of the scheme with greater realism. Questions to be considered may include, "Is it better, with the known or likely resources, to focus only on the elderly, or do the virtues of a more generalised service within a given geographic area tip the balance in that direction?" "Is a carers' support scheme the appropriate response from the team to the elderly, or is the need for respite residential care at week-ends more pressing?"

This example brings together notions of 'community of interest' and 'community of locality'. All the people in the community who are carers of elderly relatives may be conceived of as a community of interest, and, in this instance, are conceived of also as being part of a community of locality, i.e. a neighbourhood. Both usages are orthodox and serve a purpose, although noting that both usages are at work may raise such questions as "Why restrict the community of interest by the boundaries of locality?" After all, the interests of carers may be better met by crossing neighbourhood boundaries. However, these would be essentially pragmatic issues to be dealt with by the team in the light of its other process aims and values.

Obviously there are many viable carers' schemes which have not been developed in this way. Our experience is that using the kind of management process outlined here fosters the sense of working *with* the community and makes it likely that other energies or resources will be mobilised by the nature of the process itself. Current orthodox social work, however sensitively handled, tends to foster the sense of doing things 'to' or 'for' the community, with resulting problems of dependency and learned helplessness on the part of consumers. The attitude of mind which lies behind the process described here is one which can inform all areas of work.

2. **To engage in identifying community resources for care.**

"It became readily apparent that there are relatively few resources within the Stonybrook area and that particular estates and areas seemed especially isolated and uncatered for, despite their high proportion of elderly. Further, from talking to the home helps in the area, it was made clear to us that many of the elderly, although complaining of loneliness, were not interested in using the more traditional lunch clubs or day clubs run by Age Concern. This was mainly because they felt intimidated by, or were not used to mixing in such large groups . . . The senior social worker had already built up good relations with the staff at Stonybrook Lane family group home. They were keen to extend the use of the home during the day time and suggested that we could use their home as a location. The staff were also very keen to do the cooking." (Newcastle Social Services Department 1986.)

Thus a group of three social workers in Newcastle began a small but significant scheme designed to foster a neighbourhood network of care. No additional large scale resources were needed — only lateral thinking by people in a number of different situations.

For such initiatives to emerge social work teams need to allow their members 'thinking time' as well as 'activity time'. *What* to think about is implicit in the above — we would identify the elements more formally as:—

a) examine work done by all other agencies and the manner in which it is done;

b) identify and use existing networks — that is, establish who relates to whom, about what. In particular, how do primary carers relate, i.e. household/family members, and how do secondary carers relate, i.e. neighbours, 'professionals';

c) consider, in consulation with those in your own and other agencies and those involved in the caring networks, whether more can be developed from the resources they represent;

d) record gaps in both the resource and support systems for existing networks;

e) begin to seek ways of making good deficiencies identified in (d) in consultation with those involved.

This activity identifies the potential for changing relationships between people, so that some people's needs can be met. The re-direction, or re-formulation, of people's efforts can provide a springboard for developing new or different patterns of care from those which exist. These processes are one element in the task of neighbourhood assessment. In carrying them out the team is aiming to develop preventive programmes with an emphasis on a pro-active rather than a re-active approach to problems faced by people in the community. It is probable that the identification of gaps in resources will lead to the need to seek special funding in one form or another, and it is important to recognise that this activity is not simply an end in itself. A network of carers is strengthened by working together on practical issues, especially when these are felt to be directly relevant to the carers themselves and those for whom they care. For example, should the Stony-brook group find they need money to develop or sustain the activity, it would be important for the social workers to share *that* problem with all those involved in the first initiative: the older people themselves, the home helps, the Stonybrook Lane staff, their team colleagues. Under the pressure of felt immediate crisis, it is easy to ignore this process. Subtle, or not so subtle, changes in the 'ownership' of the initiative would then result, with corresponding loss of the reciprocity on which the lateral thinking, so important at the beginning, depends.

3. To identify and review types and methods of intervention

We have said that community social work is essentially a team activity which includes not only the planning of work and allocation of tasks and roles, but also the creation of a process for reviewing their development and achievement; that is, their consequences. The manner of doing this will vary according to the aptitudes and interests of the team and the tasks being worked on. For example, one team, working for a voluntary agency on a housing estate lacking most forms of community resources, committed itself to anecdotal recording of as much of their work as possible, with little or no attempt to analyse the impact of the work for the first six months. Their choice was governed by the simple fact that they did not know in advance what would be significant. At the end of six months the team re-read their narratives and used them to begin to 'flesh out' other statistical and demographic information that had been gathered about the estate, adding considerable depth to their area needs assessment. This can be a helpful approach to project work and, over time, a team will draw upon elements from conventional reviewing processes in established methods of work — groupwork, casework, community work — creating a recording and reviewing system which they feel to be relevant and effective in their situation. The essential requirement is that recording and reviewing happen, and that they happen within a format which is common to all team members. The content of recording needs to include:—

a) initial statement of aims;

b) statement of who is to be involved — team colleagues, community leaders, local residents, workers in other agencies, and so on;

c) statement about how others are to be involved and why, by — face to face contact, formal/informal meetings, written communication by team members working alone or in pairs/trios, and so on;

d) record of how the above decisions were reached — solely within the social work team, through engagement with informal carers, inter-agency meetings, negotiations with people receiving services, etc.

Our experience also suggests that teams need to agree realistic time scales, with the pace of development manageable for all those involved. However, accurate time scales in this kind of activity are extremely difficult to forecast. It is probably more helpful to agree when work will be *reviewed* rather than when a particular task will be *finished*. The 'realism' of timescale, however, is frequently a difficult balancing act — if tasks are not achieved on time team morale will diminish and further work then suffers. The more carefully distinct phases in the work can be identified, either in advance or as the work develops, the less likely this is to happen.

As part of the reviewing process, it is important to assess within the team, with other agencies and with those involved in caring networks, whether aims could be better achieved by other forms of intervention/activity. Questions to be considered include:— How is time allocated to different activities: one to one work, groupwork, indirect work, team meetings, work planning? Is this the most productive use of time? How can the allocation of time be changed?

4. **To seek ways of sharing in the social problems of the community.**

Let us return to the situation of the Edwards family, described in Chapter 2.

On the second day of the clean-up the caseworker was just leaving the Edwards' house in his car when a lady down the street yelled something at him:

> "I wondered who it was and saw a lady I did not know standing on her front step yelling, presumably at me. I stopped the car and walked back to her. 'What you helping them buggers for?' She yelled. 'They're more trouble than they're worth. It's buggers like them give the street a bad name.' I asked her what she would do to them. 'I'd put the buggers out,' she said. I asked her where she'd put them and pointed out that you couldn't just put kids out on the street. 'I'd put them on their own somewhere worse,' she answered. I told her everyone had told me this street was the worst place in the town. Having gone around that circle, she stopped yelling and we talked for a bit more about what it was like living in Graham Street, and I challenged her quite hard on why she wanted the Edwards to stay the way they were. I went on to say we wanted the whole street to see that the stigma belonged to all of them and not just the

Edwards, and so everyone had to do something. While I did not feel she accepted what I said, she did listen and begin to understand it."

A vivid account, recorded by Holder and Wardle (1981), of one worker beginning to share social problems with the community. It is rare, perhaps, for a worker to have such an opportunity, but worth noting the choice the worker made — "I stopped the car and walked back to her". He could have driven on. 'Sharing social problems with the community' carries with it all the complications we indicated in discussing the first characteristic process aim of engaging communities in setting aims and objectives. Many of the same processes and strategies are appropriate, and can only be achieved by a commitment to openness and straight talking. The straight talking will, of course, be a two-way process and part of the professional task is to ensure that there are forums where this can happen as constructively as possible. This may mean using existing meetings such as lunch clubs or groups of all kinds, or it may mean taking care that, when a new initiative is being planned, all appropriate parties are involved and have an opportunity to identify problems, objectives and review methods.

The initiative with the Edwards family required work within the agency itself — co-ordinating casework, groupwork, neighbourhood work; with other agencies — tenants' associations; as well as with the family. The agency members only made progress when they recognised *and shared with all these other groups* that the problem was not only that the Edwards family were dirty, delinquent, and anti-social, but that almost all the other groups had a vested interest in them remaining as they were. Other residents felt safe as long as the Edwards' family standards were worse than theirs; agencies noted them as one form of justification for their existence. The work, therefore, needed to be shared in family meetings, neighbourhood meetings and interagency meetings, and within those meetings a new definition of the problems had to be both negotiated and worked on.

At the other end of the spectrum, a social services department, seeking to maximise care in the community for elderly and handicapped people, began by formulating its own departmental strategy and sharing it with all other relevant agencies, both voluntary and statutory, elderly people themselves, and their carers. Two years later, a complex series of meetings at all levels has led to a clear policy governing the use of residential and day care resources and the beginning of a similar policy-formation in relation to community nursing, health visiting, home help service and social services department fieldwork services. At either end of the spectrum the work processes involved are identical even though the people were different: relating to service providers and users working together to identify needs, clarify expectations and generate resources.

5. **To engage in negotiating boundaries with other organisations**

Social work teams, seeking to promote community social work, are likely to be faced with the need to develop and extend negotiating skills which have previously been used only in a relatively narrow way. Most caseworkers, for example, will have negotiated on clients' behalf with fuel boards or housing departments and/or will have negotiated the re-entry of difficult adolescents into their own families. Teams will need to acquire knowledge about boundaries of work and levels of authority within other agencies. Less formally, there is the need for the 'sixth sense' of where power lies in practice as well as in theory, who influences whom, what is open to negotiation and what isn't. Planning needs to use both the formal and informal levels to see a new project started and progress. Failure to do so can be costly; there are many examples related to the location of hostels for almost all categories of people with special needs, which have had major difficulties because of failures to consult effectively with local residents.

Teams need to give thought to the scale of a proposed project and to identifying key figures to be consulted. A group for people recovering from mental illness may require little more than the allocation of worker time within the team to negotiate with a local vicar and/or parish council for the use of a church hall. Perhaps parishioners represent potential resources, or maybe the group's existence is threatened by a parish group choosing to change its meeting day. By contrast, a team seeking to develop joint working with a primary health care team with the aim of maintaining more frail elderly people in the community needs to recognise that a great deal of preparation time will be required. The aims of the project must be validated with senior management in both agencies, middle management must be satisfied about common referral and assessment procedures, practitioners and administrative staff in both agencies must be prepared to accept assessments and recommendations from new sources, voluntary agencies consulted about alternative referral procedures, and so on. Similarly, a delinquency management scheme, aiming to divert adolescents from custodial sentences or local authority care, will require negotiations with the magistrates, their clerks, the police, the probation service, and acceptance by social workers of additional scrutiny of recommendations in enquiry reports.

In any such developments the team members' actions will blur current job demarcation between the agencies. Task sharing will be part of the negotiation and contract building programme. Together with other people, team members will be searching for new solutions to problems, and finding these will be inherently but positively critical of the tasks as currently performed.

To suggest changes in the prevailing patterns of care can be a risky business. Not all management levels of all agencies will be receptive to such positive criticism in the early stages. But a linking process between agencies will be developing, and will become visible as partnership projects emerge and are seen to be effective. This needs to be communicated to appropriate management levels so that criticism is perceived in the appropriate context. It may also require clarification of official boundaries within each agency, so that protocols are not offended. This process is helped considerably if clear liaison procedures are established and publicised: for example, identifying named individuals as carrying that responsibility, or establishing regular meetings for that specific purpose. However it is done, the liaison work will entail the team in negotiating the role and limits of their own organisation, thus helping to demistify the agency and keep it more accessible to others.

6. To engage in negotiating boundaries between different parts of the organisation

Obviously the skills required to incorporate this characteristic into the team's work are closely related to those discussed in the preceding section. However, it is important here to start with the team itself.

All the members of the team need to be aware of the boundaries relative to each other. This is not to talk of job demarcation, but to emphasise what each team member can expect from the others from time to time. While this is being achieved, the collective relationship of the team to other parts of the department can be established. It is necessary to define clearly the areas of activity which the team can control by negotiation, and the areas which are clearly controlled by others in the organisation. This cannot be done effectively without the team initially having been involved in developing an approach to team building. Through these processes the team can begin to establish goals. The interactive processes of team building, participative management and goal setting, contribute to the clarification of relevant issues and a definition of the work which needs to be done. This, in turn, allows the team as a whole to begin the process of intervening and interacting with other parts of the organisation from a position of strength, as a group, and from a knowledge base which makes its organisational position difficult to ignore.

Team members need to recognise and value the nature of their position within the agency. It is area office staff in social services departments who are usually at the interface between the organisation and the rest of the community. It is, therefore, the progenitor of most of the work of the rest of the department.

The team does not, however, control all the resources likely to be demanded by the community it serves and is, therefore, inextricably involved in negotiating at all levels within the organisation.

Boundaries can be erased unwittingly — the development of the carers' support scheme described earlier could be considered to be infringing the domain of domiciliary services. If so, the team will need to consider whose task it is to negotiate flexibility around that boundary. The staff at Stonybrook family group home were preparing meals for the elderly; would such a modification require negotiations with management and the unions? Who decides whether it is necessary to do so?

As a team enlarges its repertoire of methods of work to include groupwork, systems intervention work, community development work, as well as casework, roles will become blurred. The team must monitor this process and communicate it through the management structures so that it is understood and appreciated. Job descriptions may need to be re-written to accommodate this more flexible way of working, administrative systems modified to accommodate it, levels of autonomy re-defined. The function of team meetings will be changed by these demands and their increasing importance must be communicated to middle management and above. Similarly, the changing emphasis of work must also be communicated, since the development of successful preventive work can lead to problems of staffing levels when a department allocates staff by weighting allocated statutory cases at the expense of other work.

Boundaries continue to be explored in the seventh, eighth and ninth key characteristics.

7. **To work out ways of sharing work in the team**

Shared work is a difficult principle to put into practice. In post-war social services, work has been received as individual referrals, parcelled out to particular grades of workers. Typically, CQSW workers are given the difficult statutory field work cases, and other staff receive work suitable to their status, position and assumed skill level. Residential and day care workers are set to work with the people seen to require this type of institution: the relationship between the difficulty of the task and the training of the workers being less explicit, or even unconsidered. Such approaches assume that the needs in the community are best defined only as individual needs. It also assumes that people's problems can be defined in terms of types of person, and further assumes that qualification and job titles demarcate satisfactorily who should do what. Practitioners engaged in community social work do not accept these assumptions but argue that social work interventions are directed at changing relationships and the patterns of relationships, as well as the provision of goods, services and care.

The prime implication of this is that a team seeking to develop community social work must foster a sense of collective responsibility for all requests for work received by the team. In practice, most teams involved in community social work adopt a group process for the allocation of work. This is not a matter of the team meeting as a group while the leader hands out work, but of team members being actively involved in preparing the requests for staff time for presentation to the meeting, and ensuring that appropriate administrative follow up work is done. It also requires team members involved in or wishing to initiate project work presenting information or ideas about the demands of that work through this meeting, and sharing policy development with the whole team. This process engenders a sense of reciprocal accountability and responsibility, and opens the way to work being carried out by various combinations of workers according to available time, the nature of the task, and interests, skills and aptitudes of workers, rather than on the basis of formal job descriptions. It is also possible for workers to bring work back to this forum as demands or circumstances change. In reviewing work in this forum, alternative strategies or resources can be identified. Fuller, more detailed, reviewing of projects may well require that team meeting time be set aside for this.

As the two-fold principles of team responsibility for the management of work and mutual accountability for its achievement become established, in practice the actual sharing of work develops its own momentum. It may take the form of duos or trios of team members constituting sub-teams for particular projects, or individual team members working with colleagues from other agencies and local residents, or the growth of peer consultancy where the expertise of particular team members is drawn upon by others without the 'experts' themselves having to be directly involved in the work. Such strategies also encourage the development of alternative supervision systems so that group or peer supervision becomes more common. Experience has shown that, where this kind of cluster of approaches has developed, it is rare for work or developments to be lost simply because of staffing changes within the team. Commitment to the work runs at a very high level and job satisfaction is correspondingly increased.

8. To set up ways of recognising and recording work

At first sight this objective could well appear redundant — 'work' is what is defined by statute, comes through the door or is referred over the telephone. In our experience, teams which accept that definition of work spend a great deal of time assessing whether an individual is eligible for a particular set of services, and under-value time spent either in rendering those services acceptable or in managing those situations where an individual does not 'qualify'. We would argue that an effective definition of work begins with and includes the process of undertaking a thorough assessment of need, and only when this is completed is consideration given to which courses of action begin to meet the need. For example, an elderly person who suffers a stroke may well be eligible for a whole range of services — home help, day care, full admission to residential care — but the primary need could well be one of finding ways and means of re-vitalising a pre-existing network of friends and family. If that need is recognised as primary, then 'work' for the social workers becomes a matter of facilitating change in the network to achieve that end. Such a course of action may well be more useful and satisfying to that elderly person than a whole range of other services.

Similarly, most social workers are only too well aware of the offending adolescent who has 'qualified' for a care order, but where work invested in achieving that outcome does not meet the real needs of alleviating unsatisfactory family systems or modifying individual behaviour patterns.

When a team begins to work in this way the implications of what then is defined as work are considerable. It includes time spent in meetings, 'talking around' individual and community situations in an atmosphere which encourages lateral thinking. Information which would be considered peripheral within a narrow casework or strict service delivery orientation becomes much more important and needs to be recorded in an appropriate and accessible way. Records need not only to be kept but analysed and understood. Teams need to develop their own skills in monitoring their own performance. Time spent in 'worry work' provoked by a particular situation is likely to be productive and creative but time spent in simply corporately worrying about the same situation can be pathological. For example, it can indicate an inadequate response to a spell of very heavy pressure because of the volume of referrals. If it is recognised as the latter, and it happens to all teams, strategies can be devised to cope with the real issue. The team needs to record its discussions and gradually accumulate a pool of strategies and resources which can help. All this is work.

As the team re-defines its work so the demands upon the administrative support staff will change. It is important that the administrative staff who will be involved in collecting and collating information are regularly part of the team meeting. Only by being so involved can they appreciate the reasons for information gathering and contribute to devising the most effective ways of doing it. Similarly, the demands for recording all the work of the team will require changing skills on the part of secretaries. Some or all of the meetings will need to be noted, and skills developed or re-applied in new settings so that essential points are recorded; both social workers and administrative staff may need training in the use of new equipment. Such developments are a tangible demonstration that the creation of flexible, responsive, needs-based services is a whole-team responsibility and not simply within the province of the 'front line' social worker.

9. To set up decentralised locally autonomous management procedures for allocating task responsibilities

Many of the processes mentioned in earlier sections are equally applicable here. Group allocation, peer group supervision, effective engagement with the community, all contribute to the growth of local autonomy. For local management to flourish and 'manage', as distinct from having a consultative function, will require considerable boundary negotiation both within and beyond the agency. As with the other objectives there is no one way, no 'right' way of achieving this. Those departments where de-centralisation and 'patch' working have been established as policy may give their workers more formal opportunities to cross boundaries, blur job descriptions and so on, but it would be dangerous to assume that such a step is a prerequisite for change. The development of good practice within a preventive framework generates its own momentum for change. The Stonybrook family group home project, mentioned earlier, has created a new resource which is likely to be locally managed by those using it, working in it and working to it. Day centres can generate their own steering groups, involving users and 'professionals'; residential child care resources can come to fall within the ambit of a delinquency management programme; the use of local facilities already owned and controlled by tenants' groups creates a 'de facto' locally autonomous management situation. These evolving strategies are equally as powerful and valid as a centrally established policy and many have, in time, generated major policy changes.

However the development of local autonomy is approached, the guiding principle should be that those affected by decisions should be party to the decision-making process, and that problem-solving for users comes first. Organisation and management practice depend upon an objective understanding of users' needs. This applies to the community social work team itself. That is, in the same way that 'clients' and users of social services should be involved in the decision-making process of the service, so too should the 'front line' workers in relation to their own management systems. In short, managers should practise the quality of relationships with their staff that they expect staff to maintain with others. The implications of this will be developed when we come to examine organisational issues in Chapter 6.

Conclusion

We think these nine characteristics are general to community social work. Obviously there will be differences in detail depending on the specific work problems and situations faced over time: they will evolve as circumstances change and as workers become more effective in influencing change in their own social situations.

Moreover, while the team is engaging in and analysing these processes they will also be drawing on, re-formulating and refining their understanding of 'community social work.' In Chapter 4 we discuss the major ways in which community is defined and consider the problems of defining community social work.

Chapter 4

Community Social Work:
Your Team's Definition

Introduction

The ideas that people have shape their views of what they see and the people they relate to. So here we review the problem of defining community social work, and the different ways in which community has been used as a concept.

The problem of defining community social work

At first glance there simply is not a problem of defining community social work. The Barclay Report defined it, and there have been several subsequent formulations making broadly similar statements:—

"Community social work is concerned both with responding to the existing social care needs of individuals and families and with reducing the number of such problems which arise in the future. Its actual form will vary greatly from place to place and time to time, but its underlying rationale is more enduring.

"It rests, as we have made clear, upon a recognition that the majority of social care in England and Wales is provided, not by the statutory or voluntary social services agencies, but by individual citizens who are often linked into informal caring networks.

"This recognition leads to a widening of the focus of social work attention. The individual or family with problems will of course remain the primary concern of social services agencies. The solution, easing or prevention of individual or family problems is and remains the reason for the existence of personal social services agencies. But the focus will be upon individuals in the communities or networks of which they are part. There has been a tendency for social workers to see their own clients in sharp focus against a somewhat hazy background in which other people were somewhat less than life-sized. Community social work demands that the people who form a client's environment are seen for what they are or may be — an essential component of the client's welfare.

"Social workers have already moved from a focus upon individuals, or mothers and children, to see people as members of families. What community social work demands is that the circle of vision is extended to include those who work, or might form a social network into which the client is meshed. Social workers have to be able to take account of a variety of different kinds of networks."

(Barclay Report 1982, p.202)

Another approach has been to identify what community social work is not (Henderson and Thomas 1985): taken in conjunction with the Barclay definition, this can make a clear and succinct statement. So, community social work is not:—

a) the practice of a 'community social worker';
b) the odd project/group/volunteer tacked on to a case oriented team;
c) community work;
d) just about informal care networks;
e) solely about a shift in the balance of provision between local authority services and the voluntary sector — though partnership in joint planning is crucial.

But it is:—

a) the attempt to move away from a model of professional cure of individual problems;
b) the move away from a service delivered by a group of otherwise anonymous workers organised in large (to the consumer) overly bureaucratic area teams;

c) the move away from a service which is organisationally and professionally over-compartmentalised;

d) the move away from a service where the professionals are known only to 'clients' or other helping professionals in the area.

All these points are consistent with the theoretical perspective of this book as a whole. A new term such as community social work will inevitably be interpreted in many ways. So as to establish a clear definition, we need first of all to identify the kinds of distinctions listed above as a preliminary step.

However, any expansion of a definition is only useful if it helps answer such questions as "But what exactly do I do, to 'move away from a model of professional cure of individual problems'?" The rest of this book provides answers but even so there will be much still to understand which no definition can explain. Definitions are only windows on to the world.

We have stated that a team's definition of community social work will be built to fit their own circumstances. This approach is found troublesome by those resistant to adopting community social work: it is part of the process of innovation that those who oppose it demand incontrovertible proof of its effectiveness, even though the validity of the status quo is unproven.

This opposition is also manifested in the demand for a comprehensive definition. Unfortunately, the nature of innovations is such that the certainty of a priori predictions and definitions cannot be guaranteed. To change deliberately requires an act of faith. Our 'clients' confront us all the time with this resistance to change, and we, like them, will probably only move because it becomes inevitable, or because the status quo is so unbearable we have to take the risk, or because we are offered the support of a trusting set of relationships.

We should not underestimate the difficulty of changing to a community social work orientation. It is the sort of difficulty people 'out there' in the community find in changing their attitudes and behaviour, a difficulty that some would argue has largely rendered social work impotent from the beginning. What community social work has in its favour is this very impotence of much orthodox social work. Furthermore, to believe in the possibility of holding on to a no-change status quo is to believe in a myth. Being a part of community social work means accepting the challenge of being part of an ever-changing social work agency. The agency must change to make itself relevant to an ever-changing social world. This involves a continuous process of constructing definitions of its purpose in the community, in partnership with that community.

As a step in understanding the facets of community social work it is useful to examine one of its key terms, namely 'community'. The different assumptions made about community inform the way people behave and the way social workers practice. We review here some of our own experiences of discussions about community and offer a critique of the ways it is used. This discussion is intended as an aid to a team's own process of arriving at a sufficient understanding of community and community social work.

What is community?

Robert Pinker has written of 'community':—

> "It is one of the most stubbornly persistent illusions in social policy studies that eventually the concept of community — as a basis of shared values — will resolve all our policy dilemmas. The very fact that this notion is cherished from left to right across the political spectrum makes it highly suspect. . . . It seems that when our policy-makers reach an intellectual impasse they cover their embarrassment with the fig leaf of community." (Barclay Report 1982.)

It is not our intention to rebut such well expressed cynicism. We suspect that the hunt for a 'real' meaning of community is an illusion. It may be the case that it is a concept which social workers would do better not to use, but the stubborn persistence of the concept marks intellectual, emotional and practice needs which will not be met merely by arguing down the concept.

Community of locality

The notion of community as locality, and the re-organisation of social work units on this principle has been extensively recorded in the discussion of 'patch' approaches and constitutes the dominant organisational model for community social work (Hadley and McGrath 1980 and 1984). This section does not attempt to justify, evaluate or criticise this approach. 'Patch' is an illustration of the ways an assumption of community of locality enters into attempts to define community social work, and an illustration of the benefits which it is believed will accrue from practices based on this assumption. The following quotations from our own working party discussions illustrate this approach.

a) "The question is often asked, 'Can community social work only be applied to easily indentifiable estates?' Experience indicates this is not the case although the ratio between size of patch to social workers will affect the style of community social work applied."

b) ". . . Barclay stresses that community social work depends upon an attitude of mind 'which regards members of the public as partners in the provision of social care'. Partnership, however, requires a solid bedrock and it is important for social workers to see their neighbourhoods for what they are . . . It is only to be expected that public motivation towards social work . . . will be found to vary from place to place."

c) "I think locality based work is primary . . ."

The foregoing statements from three different practitioners of community social work show different aspects of the central position of community as locality in their thinking and practice. It is not a simple or monolithic assumption, but is, nonetheless, a recognisable and major element in the network of ideas used to describe practice.

In the first statement, it is *as if* community social work is a recognisable methodology which can only be operationalised in geographically bounded 'patches', and the issues will be over what *kinds* of patches, i.e., patches other than estates. In the second statement the idea of partnership as a central element of community social work is treated *as if* partnership is something that goes on in 'neighbourhoods', and as something that will vary from 'place to place'. The implication is that *locality* and *place* are of critical importance.

The idea of community based on locality enters into the definition of community social work in several ways. Although a team making the transition to community social work may seek to leave this use of the concept behind, it is almost bound to return and re-appear in obvious and not so obvious guises. For example, other agencies or other parts of the social work organisation may well assume this use of the concept in its practice and policy.

The following further statements from practitioners illustrate the advantages for social work practice of being more precise about locality based models of community.

d) "(Thus) it is our view that for team members the search for clarity in understanding their catchment area is crucial to matching needs and resources, directing services to those most in need . . . For a social work area office, the notion of catchment area is significant. The ordering of priorities, allocation of tasks and limitations as to jurisdiction are all determined with this in mind . . . Therefore, it is first and foremost that a fieldwork team should direct its attention to its neighbourhood."

e) "The local knowledge available to social workers has been a largely untapped source of placing the people we deal with in a context which makes the work we do with them both appropriate and real for them."

f) "I felt quite confident by going local two things would occur . . . you make more contact with more people . . . you become aware of how the local state operates in the locality . . ."

g) ". . . in my experience workers who have worked on a locality basis have made themselves much more vulnerable and open to local groups of people and to agencies when negotiating with agencies, and are the better people for doing extended team work across areas because they have learned those skills . . ."

The foregoing statements provide a small illustrative sample showing the range and depth of implications which the principle of community as locality often carries for social work practice. So, understanding community qua locality is viewed as crucial for "matching needs and resources"; providing a context in which social work can be experienced as more "appropriate and real"; ensuring "more contact with more people"; and making social workers better at "extended team work". In short, organising social work practice around the principle of community as locality may be viewed as having many varied, important, and desirable consequences for that practice and its practitioners.

It seems useful to give a short sample of some of the critical responses of our working party to community as locality before going on to discuss alternative approaches.

h) "With the adoption of a community social work approach it is likely that the notion of catchment area will prove to be a mixed blessing. . . . Perhaps of most importance, how residents view their community is unlikely to fit neatly with area boundaries that are designed to meet administrative and staffing requirements . . ."

i) "Where you are responsible for this geographical area it can make people very inward looking and very parochial and it can undermine the crossing of boundaries and development of work on issues like race awareness . . ."

j) "If, for example, we were thinking in terms of powerful pressure group activity to get more firm, reliable, respite care for carers of the elderly, they'd be much more likely to be effective if organised beyond the neighbourhood. It is often unlikely to get enough people who are caring relatives in one neighbourhood . . ."

Such critiques show the limitations of identifying exclusively with locality, but do not detract from the significance of the differing applications of locality for practice, as we argue later.

Community as locality has been a major organising principle for those innovative practitioners who have developed community social work as a distinct approach, and who informed the Barclay Report and subsequent debates (for e.g. Hadley and McGrath 1980). Any team beginning to make the transition to community social work will need to be aware of this, and will have to engage in the same issues about the nature of community. It is likely that the kind of comments made in the foregoing quotes from practitioners speaking for and against the principle of locality will re-occur within any social work team making the transition to community social work.

Community as defined by common interests

The other main use of community is to refer to community of interest. The Barclay Report defined this notion of community in relation to a person who

> "is likely, in addition to his local connections, to have a number of relationships that matter to him with people and institutions outside a circumscribed geographical area. He may share with such people a particular social disadvantage or handicap, or a common interest based on work, leisure activities, or attendance at the same doctor's surgery . . . The allegiances he feels to people and groups outside a local area may well be as important, or more important, emotionally, than those within it. We use the term 'communities of interest' to describe these networks of relationship."
>
> (Barclay Report 1983, p.xiii)

The interplay between the ideas of community of interest and community of locality has its counterpart in other polarities such as genericism versus specialism. For a social work team, these issues are likely to be part of the process of developing partnerships with other people, groups and organisations in the community. Sometimes there will be an adversarial quality to the relationship between the two approaches to community. For example, a worker from a voluntary agency working in partnership with a social work team organised largely on a 'patch' basis remarked rather angrily at a team meeting:—

> "The community of shared concern or interest is as important a locus for social work as the community of shared locality. The team is in danger of ignoring this dimension. . . . I confess to prejudice against neighbourhoods, wards, villages. Sociologists' love affair with neighbourhoods cooled off twenty years ago. Community workers dropped them ten years ago. Social workers have just discovered them!"

Irrespective of the 'truth' of that worker's view, or the 'truth' of the view to which he was responding, the social work team will have to engage with competing perspectives on the priority to be given to differing views of community.

In the same discussion, a 'patch' proponent responded to the voluntary agency worker by saying:—

> "I feel that, to some extent, the community of interest thesis is geared towards care rather than issues. . . . Maybe when talking about care, and people looking after relatives, then kinship and shared interests remain most important. I think when talking about issues, when talking about whether there is a chemist nearby, or what to do about vandalism, then neighbourhoods can be very strong. We should not just look at neighbourhoods in terms of care, but in terms of issues and in terms of services and resources."

The interchange between these two workers is a sample of the kinds of debates that have to go on both within a team, and between a team, the people it works with and other relevant organisations, as it goes through the process of defining its approach to community social work. So, for example, a team may, because of its base in the locality, be particularly well fitted for developing certain kinds of neighbourhood resource for dependent elderly people. But that same form of organisation may be less well fitted for responding to the demands made by a fluid delinquent group which crosses locality boundaries, and constitutes only a short-term, temporary community of interest. The social work team will have to consider and continue to reconsider the notions of community which govern its practice and priorities at any one time. The opposition between community of interest and community of locality may be only an 'illusion of opposites', which, once understood, can then be used to develop more complex interactions between the team and its communities. (See Chapter 8, "The Search for a Synthesis".)

In Chapter 3 we said that the identification of community resources was a crucial characteristic activity of community social work teams. This area of work underlines the complexity of taking an 'either/or' approach to community of interest and of locality. We now pose another approach to 'community'.

Community as shared experience of oppression

Another worker participating in the team discussion quoted above complained of the "under-representation of women and non-representation of black people and members of ethnic minorities," within the social work organisation and its community. He argued that the social work team should be engaged in developing more and more genuine partnerships with women's interests groups, black organisations, non-professional local government workers and so on. These groups were being viewed as communities of interests which were also *oppressed* communities. Abrams (1980) has argued that traditional communities, such as mining communities, developed out of experiences of oppression. Similarly, the characteristic forms of oppression experienced by women, or blacks, or non-professional staff are such that these groups form a certain kind of community of interest.

Here, the identification of this particular kind of community of interest grew out of the social work team's efforts to engage with, and conceptualise about, the different groups of people to which it had to relate. However, the team found it very difficult to take on separately all the characteristic interests of those oppressed communities. The team could no more do that than, say, a black action group could take on board all the special interests of women, even while recognising their shared experience of oppression, without putting its own identity in jeopardy and hence losing its essential utility. The outcome of this understanding is the development of a more complex view of the social work team's task as that of facilitating interchange within an often diverse network of oppressed communities of interests, in the context of the continuing process of all the team's activities, rather than as a separated-out and singular task. In this way, the concept of community, as it applies to practice, becomes even more complex.

Community as 'community sense' within a social network

The notion of 'community sense', or a sense of community, has been explicitly developed by theorists such as Willmott and Thomas (1984). It is also an idea expressed in everyday talk, deploring the loss of a sense of community, praising its resurgence, seeking to protect it if it still exists. This is a less tangible notion of community than 'locality' or 'interest' but, nevertheless, it is said to provide "an understanding of interpersonal experience without which working in neighbourhoods would be bereft of reality"; a sense of community is said to be "about the sentiments and feelings that exist within a community, and its meaning includes the social network and patterns of behaviour that sustain and reflect such sentiments and feelings." (Bennett 1980.) This is the soft dimension of community, relative to the 'hard' data expressible within the notions of community of locality, of interest and of oppression. It is relatively straightforward, for example, for a team to obtain demographic data on its locality, but far harder to identify how residents feel about a neighbourhood.

This understanding of community is often central to those wishing to change the way people feel about themselves and the groups they are part of. Increasing people's identification with an area or with their peers is often an integral part of any change in the way people unite to achieve common goals, or relate to each other to meet mutual needs. To achieve such change in perception obviously requires some understanding of people's starting points; how they perceive themselves in relation to their 'community'.

The need to juggle with these subjective definitions of community can be easily lost sight of within the technical rationality of social planning, social care, and the complex interweaving of other notions of community.

It is these subjective definitions and the needs bound up with them that partly account for the persistence of the notion of community, and its present often florid over-use. It has an essential protective role in our patterns of understanding of social reality, and this should be included with the multiple uses of the concept of community which will characterise the work of the social work team.

Social work agencies then need to recognise that there are lots of different kinds of community and that many other people and organisations are involved in defining the boundaries of community and to what kinds of community they and others belong.

Social work agencies also need to attempt to organise themselves so as to maximise their ability to understand and interweave within *all* those different versions and perceptions of community. Lastly, they need to recognise that there is a continual dynamic interplay between all the different kinds and aspects of community, so no one fixed model of organisation will ever be satisfactory.

A temporary, interdisciplinary special interest team *may* be the best way of responding to the 'care' and 'issue' needs of, say, elderly mentally impaired people at any one time, and in a particular locality. Pressure group activity to raise consciousness about, and to develop resources for, dependent elderly people may best be done on a national basis, but the development of neighbourly oversight for the older people in the case of some emergency, will require an extremely local form of organisation. A social work team will need to be able to make sense of these levels of intervention, and to engage in them without self-contradiction. What the social issues are for people may best be identified on a local basis by a neighbourhood team which really is able to hear its constituent community of locality, but will at the same time be able to organise across wider systems to respond.

This complexity is reflected in the following example:—

"The West Kensington team found they were getting increasing numbers of single homeless, mentally ill people going to bed and breakfast . . . the housing department were going up the wall about it . . . so the only way to look at it was to treat it as a general problem, to talk to other teams . . . to actually pull together voluntary organisations and health service organisations . . . to actually put the time aside rather than to work individually . . . you have to respond to the community rather than to say, 'Well it's not in our area' . . ."

The need to interweave different models of community with different models of organisation raises major research issues as to which models of each fit best with the others. Some of the crude assumptions about 'patch', for instance, have been enriched by this kind of work. But our knowledge of what modes of organisation work best within a given set of the major variables is still limited. The more extensive experience and knowledge that does exist is in the minds of practitioners, and has yet to be systematised and made available to the wider social work world.

Lastly, we need again to stress that there cannot, in principle, be a single organisational 'blue-print' which will be 'right' for all localities, part localities, different communities of interest, etc. This fluidity in the real world leads to another approach to community which formally conceptualises the actual complexities of the situation. This is the fifth way in which we consider community.

Community as punctuation of social boundaries

The theoretical dimensions of this approach to community are discussed fully in Part II; the main point here is that the boundaries drawn round a network or group of people, or a place, are, in some senses, arbitrary. Boundary making, in looking at groupings of people, is like punctuation in chains of interaction — it is the product of a decision made by a certain person or certain people. For example, London is the total urban network for some, the inner city areas minus the suburbs for others, the square mile of the City of London for others. A 'community' can mean anything from a handful of people to the EC. We say this is 'in some senses arbitrary', that is, the boundaries we draw will be governed by the purposes we have in mind.

The notion of boundary-making as punctuation provides an overarching conceptualisation for the different interacting notions of community already discussed in this chapter. Workers need to recognise that community can be punctuated in many ways for many purposes; and that such punctuations are not just the prerogative of the social work team. A team needs to be aware of different relationships between punctuations. Members of the team need to possess among them the behavioural and organisational repertoires necessary to act effectively within and across all the possible punctuations; to engage in the endless process of defining and re-defining the team's responses to 'the community' of which it is a part.

In the previous sentence, the phrase 'the community' was placed in inverted commas, to indicate that once a more complex view of community is taken, particularly the radical view just discussed of community as punctuation of social boundaries, then it becomes very problematic to state precisely what the phrase 'the community' refers to. In particular, it takes us on to the very common problem of viewing community as some kind of real natural object in the world.

Treating 'community' as a thing or a person

This is essentially a critical reminder of how we can become deeply confused intellectually and behaviourally by the way we use concepts such as 'community', or 'the team', as if they were singular entities, and in particular with human attributes. We often ascribe properties to them which properly should be ascribed only to individual people, such as beliefs, values and understanding. We speak of social work teams as *listening* to their community, or of organisations as *having* certain values. In doing this we overlook the fact that 'teams' or 'communities' are groupings of people around whom we or others place a conceptual boundary so that we can talk about them. It is then easy to develop an over-simplified picture of the *actual* social relations with which we, as social workers, are engaged. People talk about 'consulting the community' *as if* you could pop down the road and ask it something, and, by this over-simple anthropomorphisation, neglect the need to understand the complexities of actual people within their real relationships, and the multiple punctuations of such relationships. The very idea of community lends itself to this often deeply misleading 'shorthand' use.

A return to a definition of community social work

The foregoing discussion suggests that the notion of community is too nebulous and serves to complicate rather than clarify an understanding of community social work. We may do better to exclude the word, and instead endeavour to understand the patterns of relationships between the people who are in the population we are working with, and listen to how they perceive their social world, how they want it to be, how it helps or hinders them with their problems. Paradoxically, we may actually establish far better relationships with, and within, our communities, if we omit the concept of community itself from attempts to conceptualise what constitutes effective social work practice.

We conclude by proposing a straighforward definition of community social work which lists and describes certain key elements, and which we think can stand as a good enough, reasonably complete and succinct working definition of our picture of community social work.

A community social work approach:—

— embraces the functions of a whole social work agency. It is based on collaborative work in the division of labour within teams, and between teams and other formal and informal carers.

— is based on collaborative working within social work agencies and between social work staff and the networks of people with whom they work.

— involves planning to maximise effectiveness. Most care, supervision and control in the community is undertaken by parents, relatives, neighbours, other informal carers and staff in other agencies. These people's actions constitute the patterns of care and control within a community. Planning is based on an analysis of how these people relate to each other and specifically how social needs relate to available resources. Priorities and methods of work are based on this analysis and on judgments about how people should relate.

— is concerned with change in people and their relationships with others so that resources are available to those in need. A major aim is that those disadvantaged by their social networks achieve new, more advantageous relationships.

— includes the effective delivery of services to those dependent upon them. Effectiveness is characterised by accessibility and choice of services tailored to meet people's needs through their participation in decision-making about delivery of services, and the actual delivery.

— emphasises the strengths and abilities of people to engage in their own problem-solving. Practice aims to enhance rather than take over people's abilities to help each other and resolve their social problems.

Chapter 5

Developing the Knowledge and Skills of the Team

Introduction

Different teams will come to community social work from different starting points. The team will need to compare and contrast their current and future practice to identify how their skills, knowledge and organisation need to be developed. A central element in becoming a changing organisation within a changing environment is setting specific goals as part of managing change in practice.

On the paradigm we draw attention to the need to *Set up procedures for monitoring practice* and to *Compare and contrast current with future practice,* and *Identify training and organisation development needs.* We address these issues in this and Chapter 6.

The need for monitoring procedures

To be relevant to the communities they are part of, and responsible to those who fund and require social work, any team needs to strive to be as effective as possible. Explicit monitoring systems need to be built into social work activity. These systems should enable practitioners to confirm that they are reaching the people they set out to work with, that services are being delivered effectively and to provide information about the consequences of their interventions.

Since knowledge of the processes of planned social change is relatively rudimentary, the process of community social work and the transition towards it must be essentially a matter of social experimentation. This implies that a constant 'research and development' orientation within practice and organisational frameworks will be required. For example, a social work team may identify as a key characteristic of its approach to change, the need to 'engage in negotiating boundaries with other organisations'. However, the *purposes* of doing this; the *attitude* change required; the *benefits* to the people with whom the team are working; the *effects* on other activities and process aims, need continually to be monitored, both generally and in any particular instance. In this way an on-going process of review and goal setting for the team and the people with whom they are in partnership becomes central.

The monitoring systems established need to produce three types of information for decision making:

— *Workload management* information: this enables the management of the team to be based upon information about the problems tackled by the team, how much staff time and other resources are allocated and actually spent on the differing priority areas of work.

— Information about *what services* people actually receive, or *what social work interventions are applied* to particular problems. This is necessary to match forms of service and methods of intervention to priority problems identified.

— Information about *outcomes,* in terms of the match between goals set and achieved and also the consequences, intended or unintended, of social work intervention.

Establishing such management systems are part of the effective running of any organisation. (See e.g.: Hedley 1985; Miller and Scott 1984; Smale and Sinclair 1988.)

The ever changing nature of social work organisations has implications for the learning needs of their members, and the development needs of the organisation as a whole. Moving to community social work has significant implications for the basic training of social workers and other social work staff. More emphasis will need to be given to areas such as:

70

— Working across agency and disciplinary boundaries.

— Working on the margins of complex systems.

— Working in teams of peers and others.

— Working in ways open to public accountability.

— Working with devolved responsibilities and budgets.

— Working in networks of partnership.

— Working to understand sequences of behaviour that perpetuate problems and intervening to change these patterns.

However, the paradigm is focused on developing community social work in teams and within social work agencies. So here we have concentrated on staff developments within the workplace. Changes in practice may require the development of new skills and changes in organisational structure, ethos, and process. In turn, the acquisition of new skills, and their deployment, will bring about changes which carry the team further around and along the paradigm spiral into rethinking assumptions, definitions, and engagement in new activities, and so on.

Identifying new skill areas

Identifying new skill areas is a shorthand way of referring to the continuous need to be identifying and seeking to meet the learning and support needs of team members. Skill development needs to be viewed in the context of learning generally, and also in the context of organisational development. This is crucial since the emphasis is on the *team* identifying its skill deficits, not just individual members of the team.

The support needs of staff need to be given careful consideration. Developing team working will address some of these issues as will a review of supervision arrangements (see Payne and Scott 1982).

We can anticipate that a broad range of staff development needs will emerge from the process of comparing current and future practice. Throughout this book developments are identified that will have training implications for most teams. For example in Chapter 2 we stressed the need to develop team working and supervision ("Community social work and the team"); and the need for workers to develop their capacity to 'work on the run' ("Innovation and change").

There are five different modes of staff development and it is important to be clear when each should be used to develop different aspects of the team's practice skills and knowledge. They are:

a) Consciousness-raising.
b) Practice Skills Training.
c) Team Building.
d) Interdisciplinary Working.
e) Organisational Development.

Before discussing each of these modes of staff development, it is necessary to distinguish between *management functions* — defining, organising and monitoring tasks; and *staff development* — the acquisition of appropriate experience, knowledge and practice skills to carry out those tasks.

Staff in social work agencies should be clear that their support and learning activities are the *outcome* of processes of negotiation, not the means by which workers and management conduct their negotiations. Training as a way of getting subordinates or colleagues to accept 'management policy' has become commonplace in many organisations. We want to draw attention to this because it is necessary to distinguish between these different activities, not only to preserve a proper degree of awareness, and so of deliberate choice for all concerned, but also because different objectives can best be met by different modes of operation. For example, a 'training event' that is really an attempt by management to assert a particular policy is, in our experience, best set up as a negotiation from the beginning. These distinctions are particularly important in interagency working where training for, say, "the health visitor in the role of the social worker", is put forward as an alternative to getting health visitors and social workers together to negotiate how they can best communicate to achieve their separate and joint goals. Learning and support activities should not be undertaken *in place of* the negotiations and contracting which are the essential elements of working in partnership.

a) Developing support and change through consciousness-raising

There is a need for forum discussions to illustrate the different interpretations of community social work and their achievements to a wide variety of audiences, complementing the growing literature by disseminating information about practice and research. Attitudes and overall policy can then be influenced by informed discussion. For example, a local GP practice might express concern about insufficient residential care for elderly mentally infirm people in the area. The social work team could respond to this with a day workshop for all the professional and community groups involved, to raise levels of awareness about the issues involved. This would be a consciousness-raising exercise, and also be a part of the process of "seeking ways of sharing in the social problems of the community" and of "engaging in negotiating boundaries with other organisations". It would be an attempt at practising in partnership. Within such an activity the social work team would be both able to *talk about* its understanding of community social work and *enact* it within the process of the workshop. Similarly, a team could engage in such activity within its own larger organisation. Outside resource people could be brought in, to help the team become more aware of what it is trying to do in making the transition to community social work. The need for such modes of learning may arise at any point on the paradigm. It is crucial to recognise such consciousness-raising as a specific kind of development relevant to particular purposes. It is different from other kinds of learning which need to be met in other ways.

Beyond this level of consciousness-raising activity, there is the need to contribute towards developing the practice theory of community social work and its practice theory and methodology. This is achieved by workers at all levels engaging in wider networks of organisations and individuals trying to develop this orientation to social work. This book's contribution, for example, has developed out of a network of people trying to enhance their own understanding, or consciousness, of community social work practice and theory. All these aspects of learning have support functions for those attempting to innovate within their own organisations and social situations. (Crosbie, Smale and

Waterson 1987.)

Consciousness-raising is about developing people's understanding of their work, re-defining problems and identifying new ways of tackling them, not about getting people to do things differently. Other kinds of activity may have to be used subsequently to change practice.

b) Development through practice skills training

Much has been made of the need for a 'change of attitude' as an essential element in making the transition to community social work (e.g. Barclay 1982) and consciousness-raising activities are obviously an element in such attitude change. However, the notion of training for specific skills, or for implementing specific modes of service delivery, implies a neutrality of values which differentiates such learning from that involved in 'attitude change'. Skills training involves developing people's capacities in the way a carpenter learns how to use knowledge and hands. It needs to be distinguished from educating the worker, whether carpenter or social worker, in general abilities — literacy, numeracy, technology, and hand-eye co-ordination — that will equip for life generally. And this needs to be further distinguished from 'training' or 'education' designed to foster particular attitudes about how to relate to employers, colleagues, and clients. To talk of such training can have sinister overtones: to some, it is a matter of developing civic skills and responsibilities, but to others it is more like 'indoctrination'.

So allowing for such distinctions, the process of engaging in new activities to put community social work into practice will lead to the identification of specific skills requirements. Examples may include skills in assessing area needs and resources; groupwork and intergroup skills; skills in working with volunteers; skills in neighbourhood work and so on.

There is a lot of experience within social work of such training, and some awareness of how to do it effectively, and of its limitations. (See for example: Egan 1986; Henderson and Thomas 1987; and Morgan-Jones 1988.) However, we suggest that for skills training to be effective, it has to deal directly and overtly with actual social work processes. There are limitations in training staff out of their work contexts. The wider possibilities for learning within the work context are, moreover, in some respects more congruent with the basic approach of community social work, in addition to the advantages which have been identified in terms of effectiveness. (See for example Schon 1984; Smale 1983.)

c) Team building

Team working is a central element in community social work. The process of transition necessarily involves changes towards more effective team work. The literature on team building is growing.

There is a sense in which any team engaging in the process of the paradigm spiral will necessarily be engaging in team building. At the same time, just as there will be needs for individuals to develop new skills in order to proceed, so there will be a need for the team to engage in some specific learning and support activities to enhance its own process as a task group.

Community social work embraces the functions of a whole social work agency, and so it is essential that there is an effective division of labour, to make the best use of staff resources. This clearly requires a higher degree of collaborative working than so-called 'one-to-one' working which can be, and often is, maintained on a 'private practice' treatment model. It is necessary for staff to practise what they preach about partnership, planning and participation.

The need for workers to look at how they relate to each other, and to engage in processes of planned change as a work group, is sometimes seen as 'navel-gazing' and 'self-indulgence'. The fact that such 'self-indulgence' is hard and stressful is then taken as evidence of the masochistic make-up of most social workers.

We have said throughout that it is necessary for teams, however constituted, to work out together how they are going to define community social work. In addition, they need to decide how this will be carried out into new activities and learning; how they will divide their efforts and relate to each other so that the people with whom they work do not experience their help as a chronic series of well-meaning beginnings with different people.

Only then will other people experience the continuity and purposefulness that comes from a team whose members share a common professional identity.

It is important to remember that 'team meetings', team working and team building are not synonymous. These processes are integrated into the work which team members do. It is the way they do their work, not a marginal and separate activity. Consider, for example, the way in which a medical team works during an operation. Each of the members may have fairly clear special functions which are understood by everyone else. The team members' work is observable by everyone else, and responded to by everyone else as the task demands. The team works effectively as a team, but without engaging in 'team meeting' type activities. Obviously a social work team is not directly analogous to such a medical team, but the example gives some indication of distinctions which need to be maintained, and which are easily lost.

Much of the training usually met through external training course programmes would be better carried out as part of a strategy of team building. For example, work load management; assessing community needs; group work and intergroup skills are areas of development that are often new to all the team. They are best developed within the team context, not just to *aid* collaborative working, but because collaborative working is an essential part of putting them into practice.

The knowledge and experience of innovators will be needed to develop specific aspects of service delivery and change agent interventions. Teams will have to find ways of helping their members locate and access such experience and expertise as the need arises, such as through the exchanges and database of the Community Social Work Exchange (Beecher 1987). For example, the team may start engaging in 'caring for the carers' activities, and would benefit from the experience of such initiatives in other teams, and in other parts of the country. Similarly, help may be sought for such tasks as mobilising client networks; initiating different kinds of day-centre; using street-wardens; improving local participation in decision-making and so on.

Developing a team approach implies more open styles of

management and leadership. The promotion of group norms of openness where, for example, colleagues give and receive feedback on each other's performance based on joint working, are crucial dimensions of shared accountability. Open discussions of this nature do not come about simply by the abdication of traditional management roles, by the declaration of a less hierarchic system, or by introducing decentralised policies and structures. These ways of operating in agencies, and within their constituent teams, require a different form of leadership which is more, rather than less, demanding of professional skill. Senior and middle managers need training to mobilise these team leadership skills, coupled with opportunities to work out these new relationships with their colleagues within the workplace.

d) Interdisciplinary work

As we have stated, drawing boundaries round a team is an idiosyncratic, if not arbitrary, business, a matter of punctuation, as with the boundaries round community or family. Are home helps in or out? Are residential and day-care and fieldwork all part of the same team? Such questions cannot be answered in general terms, but are rightly dependent on local circumstances and local purposes. There can be no clear distinction between 'team building' and 'interdisciplinary working', since community social work centres on working in partnership with others, and such partnership always requires team building.

Interdisciplinary working is not achieved overnight: we structure interagency and interprofessional divides into our basic training and perpetuate them in post-qualifying training. Interdisciplinary seminars and short courses can help with some of these problems, but they can also do harm. Simply placing people in the same learning situation with little or no open discussion of their respective roles, professional perceptions and attitudes, can perpetuate rather than overcome interprofessional stereotypes. Changes in people's relationships need to be re-negotiated through an attempt to arrive at a shared understanding of how their respective roles dovetail to confront the whole task. Group and intergroup work training skills can be used to help with such problems. Training to equip people with the knowledge and skills required to fulfil those jobs should follow after such negotiations. We would suggest that consultancy on the ground is the most appropriate method in this area of development and learning.

Consider the implications for interdisciplinary working just across the field/residential and day-care divide. Community social work implies a continuum of care, where integrated services are seen as a way of involving informal carers and clients in the giving and receiving of services before, during, and after periods of respite or more permanent residential and day-care. The training implications of such policies are possibly enormous if it is assumed that all residential and day-care workers must blur roles with all the social workers. However, if discrete areas of expertise exist, then what will be required is a degree of collaborative working which is, we suggest, rare in current practice. Increasing awareness and skills in group and intergroup relationships will be crucial for development in this field.

e) Organisational development

Organisational development is part and parcel of the shift in thinking and practice that is involved in moving from individually based social work practice to the implementation of community social work. Both community social work and organisational development are, as we understand them, about effecting change in relationships and thus in performance, by intervening in those relationships within their normal settings, rather than assuming change will necessarily follow by working with an individual and then returning him or her to the original environment and expecting different behaviour.

If the *methods* of social work training are to be consistent with the basic assumptions of community social work, which we think they need to be, then there are areas of staff and agency development which need to be examined in a new light. The complex division of labour envisaged by a planned, integrated agency working in multiple partnerships, and changing in response to change in its environment, requires a high degree of co-operative working between managers, home helps, day-care workers, etc. To provide optimum learning, this staff and organisational development should take place *in situ,* using consultants/trainers with existing worker groups. In short, training in community social work must practise as well as preach interdepartmental, interprofessional, intergroup, and interpersonal working. If community social work means replacing the notion 'treatment for clients' with 'working in partnership' in social work practice, then it is appropriate and consistent for us to argue here that 'training workers' should be replaced by "consultancy for staff and agency development and the promotion of interprofessional and interagency working".

Chapter 6

Community Social Work and the Organisation

"Departments do not run on policy and procedures — they run on custom and practice."

The next step in the paradigm is to compare and contrast the patterns of behaviour in your organisation with those required to deliver good community social work practice. We draw on our own experience of organisations to illustrate what helps and what hinders these developments.

An organisational culture for community social work

Teams should not feel themselves distanced from the decision-making processes; from resource allocation; from budgetary control; and from planning. Nor should they feel frustrated by hierarchical structures, by having too little delegated planning and too little autonomy.

When this happens, and decision-making is distanced from the interface between agency and public, social workers run the danger of losing street credibility. Decisions tend to be taken by indirectly-accountable groups that err on the side of safety. Creative use of local resources, the potential for client to help client and the reliance on informal networks of support become increasingly difficult choices to activate. For example, the growth of panels for the allocation of social work time in child abuse cases can, at best, represent informed decision-making by a multi-disciplinary group. At worst, it can mean referring the decision to a management group, where the major considerations are uniformity of service, to appear 'fair' to competing workers, and to protect the agency should 'things go wrong'. Such trends in decision-making hinder partnership and collaboration with local groups and the people concerned. If social workers could become more sophisticated in relating practice to priority setting then the balance might be redressed; the problem is no longer how to make decisions more rational but how to improve the quality of the action. Stevenson and Parsloe (1978) concluded from their study that "so far as daily work was concerned, the fact is that the majority of team members went about their 'casework' as individuals, formally relating to their senior, 'the captain'." This type of practice lends itself to social workers becoming 'go-betweens'; a recipe for frustration all round. Within community social work, however, teams will set their own priorities and make decisions from their own informed view. Teams find this difficult to achieve in agencies designed simply for the purposes of distributing local authority resources.

Some management requirements impede social work, thus developing community social work entails a move away from organisations characterised by:—

a) a tendency for the best talent to move out of the front line and into management, liaison and supervisory roles. This leaves the least trained and/or experienced staff face to face with the customer. While this has been less of a problem in recent years, career development still demands a change from practice to management roles.

b) the spending of a significant proportion of time and money on servicing tiers of management.

c) thinking generally of users as a pressure on staff who, despite the tiers of management, still feel ill supported and ill equipped for the size of the task.

d) the majority of resources being allocated to services which come into operation after breakdown has occurred.

e) social work practice being essentially private and not open to scrutiny.

One way of moving away from such patterns of behaviour is to be able to distinguish the organisation's aims of *task achievement* from its need for *organisational maintenance*. The organisation needs to be maintained because of government requirements and local political decisions to provide services, and to ensure that employees carry out their legal duties without exceeding the department's budget. The rules and procedures that exist to meet these demands may not be the same as those needed to ensure that staff work to achieve the organisation's tasks.

Structure, form, content and task

Workers should be concerned primarily with the *content* of their work. The content of social workers' work includes his or her relationship with people predominantly outside the agency. Confusion arises when social workers, *as employees of the organisation,* are obliged to behave in a certain way. It is extremely difficult to follow procedures, to follow the correct *form* of doing work to maintain the *structure* of the organisation and, at the same time, maintain effective relationships with 'outside' people to achieve tasks jointly agreed with *them*.

The maintenance of the organisation gives a high profile to the *form* of the work, in contrast to its content or substance. In some situations those running the organisation think they know what jobs need doing, and devise detailed job descriptions which are the same for everybody apparently having the same task. They break the total task into jobs, relate these to grades and sections of workers, and require procedures to be explicitly followed to check that things are done properly according to the rules. For example, when it becomes necessary to register private homes, the appointment of a registration officer with an appropriate job description ensures the work is *covered*. Similarly, with the appointment of intermediate treatment officers, adoption officers and so on. The appointment of the properly qualified person, in a management chain, and the establishment of procedures for that person to follow are deemed to be enough to ensure the carrying out of the described task. The authority of the department's procedures is enforced by managers with disciplinary powers available in the last resort.

In terms of *content,* what the duly appointed registration officer, intermediate treatment officer, etc., actually does with whom and for what reason may be communicated to a professional supervisor, possibly to a nearby colleague, but also to nobody. The content of the work, that is, the nature of relationships with members of the public, is frequently owned only by a very small number of people or by the worker in secret.

Thus, the *form* of the work is highly apparent, and the subject of public debate, its raw material, what it is made up of, is largely unknown and even deliberately kept hidden. Even if senior managers are made aware of the content of much of the work, they rarely interfere in its 'professional' side.

It is dangerous to say too much about the content of your work when you are personally accountable for it, but it is not clear who is responsible for what. It is especially dangerous when you have no real control over events. If, at the same time, you are in a system where your chiefs are not aware of what you do but are ultimately accountable for your performance, it is hardly surprising that people hold to the *form,* and the *content* is hidden from too much scrutiny. For, to admit that the work you are doing, or think you need to do, does not accord with your job description or place in the hierarchy, is to risk censure, ridicule, or even the sack. To be silent is to be safe. If something goes wrong you are on your own, whatever the assurances from others that they accept the blame organisationally. When things go wrong, their position allows them to seek out and deal with the personal 'fault' if that is what it is, but more frequently, the outcome of enquiries into catastrophes has been yet more procedures, and organisational controls to ensure that procedures are adhered to. It is as if procedures substitute for the content of work; for the quality of the relationships between workers and the public.

Managing social work

While the quality of the content of the work (between worker and public) is crucial for achieving the organisation's tasks, the form of the work is essential for maintaining the organisation's structure. We can now ask the questions, "What is communicated upwards and downwards, and what do managers manage?"

Managers who are only concerned with organisational maintenance will focus on the form that work takes and expect workers to account for how work has been done in terms of the organisation's procedures. Since the content of social work is extremely complex, and has results which are often unclear and inconclusive, it is difficult to demonstrate clearly that such work has been responsibly undertaken.

What is communicated within the system, therefore, tends to be a description of what is being attempted rather than an analysis of impacts and outcomes, the shell within which the raw material of the work has a separate and private life. A social work agency or social services department may thus exist in two non-communicating realms at once: the visible described world of intentions and aims, i.e. the procedures or form of work; and the invisible personalised world of the interactions between staff and others, i.e. the activity and its results, or content.

The problem of child abuse illustrates this point well. Social workers are employed to protect children under the statutory powers invested in their employers. Professionally, they are trained in the law and in understanding the causes of aberrant human behaviour. There is a logic which suggests that if children are abused when social workers are in attendance, this testifies to bad social work. Ergo — change the system and/or social workers' training, and the problem of child battering will have been tackled. This logic assumes the social worker is responsible for and can control the actions of the parents, or know in advance when best to remove children from home. However, the content of the work in situations where children are battered is in all cases extremely complex; here even the wisdom of Solomon is not enough, and can only be used with hindsight. Attempts to discuss the content of the work in the press and elsewhere have been minimal.

In contrast, community social work means that the content of the work must be open to the public and to managers. We suggest that to do this, form and content must be compatible, and both must be negotiable between members of the organisations and those members of the public with whom social workers are entering into partnership. This is one way in which teams moving towards community social work will need to compare and contrast the compatibility of their organisational requirements with the requirements of effective community social work practice.

What needs to change

Social work is the product of the relationships between staff and others. Just as in management, what is done is subject to different accounts depending on who is affected by, or observing, the activity. Taking a child into care may be 'protection' or 'taking a child away', depending on whether you are the health visitor or the parent.

What needs to change is for the social work task and social services delivery to become the heart or central focus of the organisation. (A map of the whole social work and social services task is presented in Part II.) Those who do social work should be able to give a public account without being made to feel defensive, as if hiding behind agency structures. The point here is to make it possible for the whole organisation to *own* their work as it is. A next step is to make the structure able to *sustain,* rather than *define* that work. Put simply, job descriptions should follow the work not pre-define it. Managers and other support staff should provide the context within which workers get the job done, not control task achievement and sidetrack productive energy into organisational maintenance.

Community social work emphasises local definitions of need, forming partnerships with a wide range of people and building teams to provide services or to change local realities. Insofar as the present organisation of departments determines social work practice, regardless of the content of the task, community social work confronts traditional forms and structures. In this sense it is subversive. This was neatly illustrated in a dialogue between one worker and his director. The latter asked why the worker did not apply the agency's procedures. The worker responded by saying that he kept trying, but he could not make them fit the situations he constantly faced.

What we are suggesting is that some of the processes characteristic of large scale local authority departments inhibit the development of community social work. Many examples of community social work practice are maintained *despite,* rather than because of, their organisational context. Social services departments are often rightly criticised for not producing what apparently they are designed to produce. No amount of tinkering with the organisational structure will make it any different until the content determines the form instead of vice-versa.

Traditional organisational models in social services departments are based on a mixture of geographic division, client group allocation of staff and functional division of resources. They have fallen into the 'form' trap of believing what they are supposed to achieve *is* what actually happens. Privately, such beliefs can be seriously questioned. Publicly, no organisation can afford the admission and remain unchanged or credible. For this reason, any structural reorganisations are introduced and justified only by reference to better models for achieving the same overt objectives, which (if recent experience is any guide) continue to remain elusive.

Since organisational form of itself has no necessary influence on the quality of social work practice, the use of theoretical organisational models, whether managerial, political or professional, will always be incomplete. It will never be enough to 'decentralise' or re-write procedures or clarify policy. The kind of tasks needed to help the consumers in social services departments do not easily lend themselves to ready made answers. To 'go patch' may give the appearance of community social work, but unless much more changes underneath, the reality may just be a disguise, hiding traditional social work in a new smaller office.

Administrative processes

To work as a community social work department, the administrative process within a social services department must be able to:—

1. Gain an organisational view of what practitioners are doing, and of whether the practice strategies staff are using to achieve their aims are being effective.

2. Monitor the allocation of resources, both material and non-material, across the organisation.

3. Constantly re-define the tasks of the organisation based on assessments of needs, resources and priorities through the changing relationships workers have with 'clients', other members of communities and other organisations.

4. Promote the evaluation of practice to ascertain how far, and in what ways, policies and practice lead to users receiving the appropriate service, and that change has the desired consequences.

To undertake these tasks, staff need evidence upon which to make decisions and base action. This is best supplied from the *content* of the relationship workers have with users and other 'outsiders'. Thus the generation of evidence must involve all the staff in all the operational units, since all are part practitioner, part administrator, part manager, part policy maker. The division of labour around the content of the work is both intra-personal as well as inter-personal.

To create tools for obtaining the necessary evidence, attention must be given to the aims of the administrative processes set out above. For example:—

— The tools must be compatible with the ethos of community social work. If the information tools were solely numeric, this form of monitoring might ignore or obscure the content of work undertaken. It may also feed, or reinforce, an impersonal approach to colleagues and users.

— The information used in administrative and managerial processes should be usable at organisational, team and individual level.

— The information should show how far, if at all, the agreed values of the team and organisation are being applied to work in progress.

Local or departmental ethos?

If community social work practice is based on partnerships with people in significant networks, workers cannot be dominated by their own hierarchy or their own values. The way a department and its teams are organised and make decisions must take account of the reciprocal nature of the contracts forged in these partnerships. When dealing with content as distinct from 'form', goals cannot be set by *one* group of people.

It would be useful at this point to see whether the aims, direction and strategies of the organisation are marginal to the day to day work, and to see how this marginality enables workers to test the quality of the practice.

For example, let us look at the work done by different staff of the department as a consequence of a number of young families being housed in bed and breakfast accommodation.

At the executive or local authority committee level, the *form* into which this is put is something like, "What are the powers and duties of the authority which allow workers to tackle these problems?" The powers and duties enable certain activities to take place. Children at risk can be taken into care, families may be visited and counselled, and workers' expenses paid. Day care centres and foster homes may be made available and so on.

Senior managers may question housing policies, lay papers before councillors, and enter into negotiations with other agencies for support.

The *content* of field and day care activity is likely to be a response to the professional concern with difficult personal rela-tionships in families, to relationships with agencies involved such as the housing department, to income maintenance, and to other considerations like family stress, cohesion or integration, risk of violence, health factors, staff time, etc.

The *aims* of the department enshrined in policy statements may be: that preventive work should result in children remaining the responsibility of the parents; and that families are to be supported with dignity in adversity.

In this scenario the aims are not central to either the form or the content of the problem. They are 'marginal'. If a review of outcomes reveals that the bed and breakfast problem has caused children to be received into care, and that the dignity of particular families has been affected, the forms of the work have been observed and the content of the work understood. The aims of prevention, however, have not been met. They have not been considered.

The content of an individual worker's every day work is the raw material of the organisation. The legal and political require-ments are, as it were, the containers in which the raw material is placed, creating a boundary around the extent of the worker's activities. The aims are the test of whether what is done within them has satisfactory outcomes. If not, it has to be shown that the methods employed are wrong before the boundaries can be cited as the culprit. In this context it is the aims which are marginal, that is, have their reality outside the daily activity. It is precisely *because* they are *outside* that they are able to stand as tests for good practice. Were they to be part of the form or the content, they would be changed and distorted by the inevitable pressures exerted by daily life.

Unless the marginality of the aims is allowed full public discussion, the aims are never likely to be remotely realised.

Thus there is the need for space to be made available for workers to discuss the outcomes of their work, in which a critique of the forms and the causes of the content are an explicit part of the task.

Reviewing the manager/practitioner relationship.

We have said that when considering changing a social services department, it has been usual to change the structure. Community social work requires that managers do not just control activities and resources to maintain a stated form. They should also take on the support of, and be party to the content of the work done by other members of the organisation. Control of the task of the organisation is maintained by questioning the quality of the partnerships formed with other people, the appropriateness of the contract formed, and the agency staff's ability to follow through their side of the contract. It also requires beginning from the position of meeting or balancing consumers' needs, rather than of 'maintaining of the organisation'. It should be noted that 'the consumers' may be the people who 'want something done' about a problem as well as those usually described as 'clients'.

It is not surprising that people in departments have to struggle constantly to reconcile these different and conflicting possibilities. Departments have various political, managerial and professional objectives which are often in tension. Attempts to use restructuring programmes to bring about some kind of 'once and for all' change to create the 'right' organisational form are inevitably 'theoretical', based upon assumptions that the content of our work world will perhaps impinge less onerously, if we are finally, somehow, properly organised. In Chapter 2 we discussed how this stop-go perception of change in organisations can only be unhelpful.

Community social work, however, means asserting and perpetuating behaviour within an organisation which primarily solves the problems of users. Organisation and management practice should follow from weighing-up understandings of users' needs. Thus community social work requires a change in the culture and attitudinal make up of the organisation if the following attributes are not clearly developed:—

— Where there is 'no hiding place' from being actively involved in problem solving for users.

— Where people can work multi-functionally in teams, in which, to some extent, all members are managers of their own time and expertise in collaboration with their colleagues.

— People share the same values about why they do the work.

— Where change occurs by staff negotiating their roles, through the work, in a system which develops and supports change.

— Where all managers are also trainers and where training is geared to service to users.

— Where the main work centres are small scale, integrated, multi-functional teams, with as much control of resources as they can satisfactorily handle, or to which they have access.

Structural layers must be as few as possible with the emphasis on service as defined by the relationship of workers with users.

In considering such changes of emphasis account must be taken of:—

— Legal requirements, which must be undertaken despite 'client' or consumer preferences (which workers may legitimately seek to change).

— Professional ethics (which workers need to define and refine publicly).

— Political decisions (which workers may seek to influence).

— Prevailing management, union and local government attitudes and practices (which workers may challenge).

To re-organise

To re-organise a social services department so that it evolves on community social work lines, it is necessary to:—

1. Review current hierarchical patterns of behaviour which assume that those at the top define tasks, and those below carry them out. For an organisation to be consistent with the aims of community social work, the way it goes about its business must be consistent with the business it handles. A tenet of community social work is that the expectations, aims and demands of people in the community must be woven into the work of the department and that workers and managers must be equally involved.

2. Recognise the reciprocity required in relationships within the hierarchy which, at the same time, must also maintain a process of accountability and ultimate responsibility for the social work of its employees to elected members.

3. Search for a structure which accounts for people's behaviour, but which does not seek to prescribe more than the broadest boundaries round what they can do.

This view of community social work is based on the assumption that workers want to be considered intelligent and trustworthy enough to have the space they need to solve the problems created by the content of their work. This should be a publicly stated expectation of staff, who will be selected on the basis of being able to demonstrate such abilities.

Such a structure can be represented as a series of concentric circles, with council members or management committee at the outer rim; next the directorate; then middle management and support staff; and front line workers at the centre (Fig. II).

Fig. II

COMMUNITY

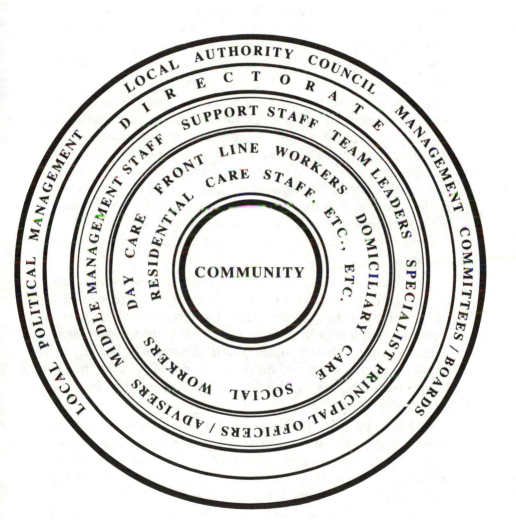

Local political management: Local Authority Council, Management Committees / Boards, Directorate. Middle management: Staff Advisers / Principal Officers, Social Workers, Day Care, Domiciliary Care, Residential Care Staff, etc., Front Line Workers, Support Staff, Team Leaders, Specialist Staff, etc.

COMMUNITY

COMMUNITY

This model illustrates our assumption that all the employees of the authority service the tasks of the front line workers.

The size of the management team outside the centre is directly proportional to the difficulty of 'managing' the boundary. Thus, the better the centre at handling the work, the easier/ smaller the task of management. The logic of this view of the structure is for more and more resources to be placed at the centre, where the work is, at the expense of the management tiers.

In practice, this structure emphasises that community social work is committed to its front line workers, using methods derived from the processes described in the paradigm. It is, therefore, appropriate for social services departments to use front line workers in local geographical teams, or in teams serving users with communities of interest; that is, at the centre of the circles where work is focused. This primary work force is serviced by other support staff from the next circle, who may develop particular specialisms or be part of the primary work force, as required.

Workers are accountable to the community in two ways. First directly, through their relationships with the people represented by the centre of the diagram. Secondly, through their organisational accountability to the small group of managers who 'live' in the next outer circle, reporting to the director who bounds the whole, with the committee on the outer rim. The committee is then accountable to 'the community' represented by the area outside the circle.

In this approach, the large cohorts of middle management characteristic of local government are portrayed as active support staff. Given the magnitude of the task now expected of front line workers, they will need all the available help. As the task of the team is clarified and resources defined, they will thus be able to absorb as much of the outer support services as overall budgets and good management will allow.

The optimum organisation will be characterised by fully self-sufficient, fully community-based, self-regulating teams, accountable to a small group of managers who report to elected members. Members may be centralised in large committees, or

94

decentralised into local groupings, or a mixture of both.

In practice, such an evolving organisation needs some indication of the tasks of individual workers. It seems to us that only three kinds of job are needed:—

— Geographically based and "community of interest" workers (front line)

— Specialist support workers (second circle)

— Managers (third circle)

Staff in all three circles are supported by appropriate administrative personnel.

It is clear that a social services department moving to a community social work approach will be re-modelled culturally and structurally by its members. We believe that departments are now doing and will continue to do this work. Often such social services departments are also changing to decentralised modes of working, and sometimes vice-versa. We believe that the implications for professional and management training are massive. Similarly, recruitment, accountability systems, work analysis and so on, have hardly been tackled as major issues. The tools for doing this work are currently being devised as departments 'fly by the seat of their pants.'

Chapter 7

Making the Transition:
Paradigm and Action Planning

The paradigm we have presented gives a general guide to the processes of community social work and to the process of transition to it. A central element is the team's need to engage in the continual construction of specific and concrete plans for change based on its own particular circumstances, team members' current assessment of the core elements of community social work, and evaluation of their own current practices. Earlier we discussed the value of drawing up a flow chart describing the steps to be taken by a team or department moving from the 'status quo' to community social work.

Used on its own this superficially attractive idea immediately presents problems. Such a linear model of the process of transition, and of practice, is inadequate and misleading. In particular it fails to describe the simultaneity of change, the arbitrariness of starting points, and the holistic, interactive nature of the process of change. The paradigm attempts to capture these aspects of reality within a conceptual model. A team which seeks to develop its practice within this framework will have to construct its own specific, step-by-step, problem-solving and change-facilitating sequences. These may vary in degrees of explicitness and implicitness, and may vary in quality and sophistication. But this general task will be an inescapable and continual feature of practice, feeding into the overall process of transition.

There is already a considerable literature of systematic approaches to designing effective sequences for problem-solving and change within organisation (for example Bennis, Benne, Chin, Corey 1976; Patti 1983). We are not concerned here with describing such approaches, but with outlining how they are involved in the process of community social work.

A community social work team will be engaged in many different kinds of activity, *all* of which will figure in any specific and explicit sequence of change. The process of transition is not restricted just to special projects or obviously identifiable innovations. All aspects of practice and management are necessarily included. Unless this is recognised, it is all too easy to perpetuate the marginalisation of preventative and project work. In many agencies community social work is developed by enlarging the department's range of work on a piecemeal basis. There is nothing wrong with this pragmatic approach; indeed it may be more consistent with an organic evolution for the department to maintain its relevance to the changing environment. But it is crucial to recognise that new areas of work must *replace* old ways of working. They cannot be added on, dependent upon the good will of workers or a temporary lull in other demands. Unless new resources are provided, new work always means giving up some parts of the old.

Any activity considered as an intervention, even within the orthodox parameters of a single 'case', will have some impact on the rest of the social systems interweaving with the team. A linear model of change necessarily leaves out of account whole aspects of the team's social situation (see Part II).

The process of social work intervention, and of the organisation of change, can be construed as the implementation of a number of sub-projects or sub-goals. The question then arises how best to organise the sequencing of these sub-goals. We can illustrate this by considering the complexity of designing, tooling-up, producing and marketing a new car. It is obvious that bodies have to be produced before they can be married up to engines and all the other components on the final assembly line. One solution is to produce large quantities of each component, and then store them until required. But this is extremely expensive in terms of space and capital. So it is necessary to have a system for planning how these different components can be produced so that they arrive at the right time in the right condition for assembly: the simple idea of 'critical paths'. This consists of working out what is unavoidably the longest set of steps which have to be taken, and then to use this as the framework for fitting in all the other essential, but not so time demanding sub-projects; it may be possible to identify some which cannot be begun until earlier ones are completed. Thus the overall time and the unavoidable order of the main steps are determined: the critical path is the sequence which can be completed in the shortest time and proceed as soon as possible. A flow-chart identifies the goal and the timescale of each step in the programme. Some steps may be quite predictable in their duration, and unchangeable, but others may be variable and open to unpredictable changes; hence some forecasting will be necessary. Combining the elements in the flow-chart with the timing forecast allows the construction of a critical path. However, it needs to be remembered that while a critical path can be constructed fairly precisely and completely in the case of industrial production, or indeed for most processes involving the production and delivery of concrete goods and services, such analyses will necessarily be more imprecise for a team engaged in the change processes of community social work.

The relation between the team's construction of its own critical paths and the process of transition (the paradigm) is akin to the relation between new model development and motor manufacturing. British Leyland has the general mission of manufacturing and selling vehicles for profit. For that general mission to continue, the organisation has continually to go through a cycle of new model development, production, marketing, sales and after-sales service. This requires sequences of linear actions which grow out of and feed into the complex interactions characteristic of the organisation and its external relations. Similarly, a community social work team will have to produce its own specific sequences of actions. These will develop out of a view of its own resources, constraints, and objectives, and will be carried out in partnership with other individuals, groups and organisations. The results will be fed back into the processes described in the paradigm.

We have illustrated the key characteristics of community

social work by describing in Chapter 3 how a social work team may "engage with people in the community is setting aims and objectives". The team could move straight from identifying this broad aim into a specific activity such as developing a support group for carers in the community, which, in turn, may lead the team into identifying new skill areas, organisational development needs and so on, round the paradigm. Explicit flow chart constructions can enable the team to evaluate all these implicit activities and to enhance the rationality of specific developments, so the team should move straight from identifying its process aim to action planning. There are several modes of flow-chart possible from the particular starting point of 'engage community'. We shall illustrate two:

— an action plan which describes the relationships between several characteristics of community social work as they would emerge in the development of a carer's group.

— an action plan which describes the actions an individual social worker will have to take in order to develop a carers' group within a team's community social work approach.

1) *"Engaging with people in the community in setting aims and objectives"* requires a wide range of more specific activities to be undertaken. For example, the team may initiate a community forum for interagency and wider issue-based discussions, within which a specific idea may emerge. The proposal could be for the team to become involved in the development of a carers' support group. This activity has to stand in relation to all the other process aims and constitutive activities of the team. The paradigm can be used to develop this understanding of the processes involved in setting and following a strategy for change.

This can be illustrated by the example of a carers' support group which developed out of a community forum, which, in turn, was an aspect of the broad process aim of engaging with people in the community in setting objectives. The community social work team's representative in that forum would respond in certain ways to the ideas developing within it, making decisions such as whether or not she should agree to her team even considering the idea, since it assumes various things about team working, delegation of responsibility, division of labour, work allocation and so on.

In other words, even the very first step in a possible linear action plan for considering developing a carers' support group assumes a lot of other processes are occurring or have occurred. The development of change could founder and flounder at this stage because of incorrect assumptions about the existence and quality of such processes. For example, it could be that the priority setting and decision-making processes in the team cannot cope with the kind of issues generated by a proposal of this sort, so it is avoided or mishandled. This, in turn, will contribute to the undermining of the aim which helped generate the initiative in the first place.

The development of a carers' support group must be viewed not in isolation but as part of other key aims of the team. These are to:—

a) engage in identifying community resources for care;
b) seek ways of sharing in the social problems of the community;
c) identify and review types and methods of intervention.

The following processes may also be necessary steps in negotiating aims and objectives with a broad spectrum of people in the community:—

a) set up de-centralised, autonomous management procedures;
b) review types of intervention;
c) engage in boundary negotiation with other organisations;
d) engage in boundary negotiation between different parts of the department;
e) set up ways of recognising and recording all work;
f) work out ways of sharing work in the team.

So, for example, despite what may be agreed in the forum and worked out in the team, unless there is some decentralisation of management decision-making, the project may fail in the process of going through a centralised management decision-making system. Alternatively, unless there has already been some work to identify and review types of intervention in the community, then this proposal may not be validated as an appropriate intervention by the agency. "We are a case-work agency," it might be argued, "not a community work agency." The same goes for all the other

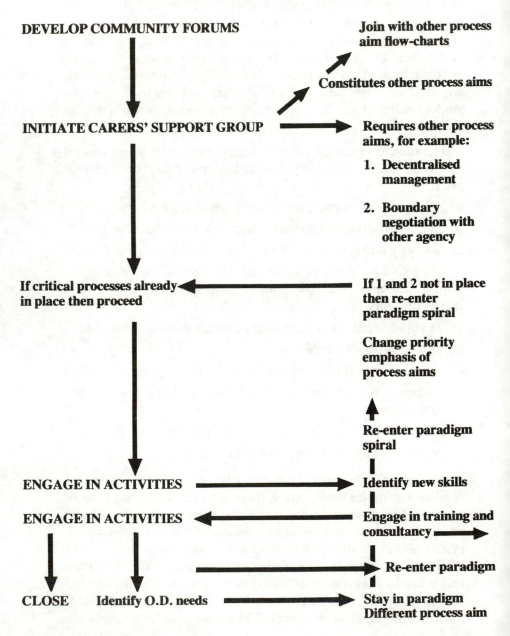

Fig. III

ENGAGE WHOLE COMMUNITY
IN SETTING AIMS AND OBJECTIVES

DEVELOP COMMUNITY FORUMS

Join with other process aim flow-charts

Constitutes other process aims

INITIATE CARERS' SUPPORT GROUP

Requires other process aims, for example:

1. Decentralised management

2. Boundary negotiation with other agency

If critical processes already in place then proceed

If 1 and 2 not in place then re-enter paradigm spiral

Change priority emphasis of process aims

Re-enter paradigm spiral

ENGAGE IN ACTIVITIES Identify new skills

ENGAGE IN ACTIVITIES Engage in training and consultancy

Re-enter paradigm

CLOSE Identify O.D. needs Stay in paradigm Different process aim process aims above, and *their* constituent activities. The product of one process aim can become part of the process of another. For example, a social worker may be able to use the team's relationship with the newly existing carers' support group to facilitate the group's intervention in seeking some boundary change between the team and the local GP practice. This is another way of talking about how an understanding of relations between the general steps of the paradigm and the team's own view of the key characteristics of community social work is necessary for identifying potential resources in a network of change. Figure III is a diagrammatic version of some of these relationships.

2) *An action plan for a specific activity: a carers' group*. The origin of the idea for a carers' group will affect the elements that need to be considered. The idea may grow out of a community forum, where some form of research about local need had taken place, leading to the proposal. Such 'research' may have been more or less sophisticated, but nevertheless provided the basis for identifying an unmet need in the community. Alternatively, it could be that a social worker initiates such an idea based on her own interest in group work, and a set of referrals where it seems obvious that carers of dependent relatives could contribute to, and benefit from, such a group. Successful innovations may originate in many ways, and from any of several parts of the social systems involved, including the individual initiative of a social worker. There are no obvious hard and fast rules as to which origin is 'best', but different origins imply a different design for the step-by-step sequences which will be most effective in bringing an innovation to fruition. (See Stocking 1985.)

The elements of a flow-chart for planning a carers' group starting from a community forum, or from an individual social worker, will be different while having many features in common. For example, the community forum may document the need, but not translate that knowledge into an effective innovation by failing to identify local resources such as people actually committed and skilled enough to follow it through. The members of the forum would have to include in *their* flow-chart the task of locating and engaging such people. They might seek to do this jointly with the community social work team, but should be cautious of believing the task is done if the team as a group approve the proposal. Groups will readily assent to the value of an idea without actually committing a member to action. The flow-chart of work with the community forum must include such issues of process if it is to be effective.

Alternatively, the individual social worker may fail to include in her action plan the need to negotiate some of the workload issues with her team colleagues, thinking, perhaps, that agreement from her senior is enough. The innovation may then flounder because of lack of referrals from colleagues; colleagues with low commitment to the idea consequent upon the innovator's failure to involve them may communicate this covertly to clients, who then do not respond to the proposal despite their need, and so on. The way in which innovations succeed and fail are often less to do with any general fact about where the initiative begins in the structure of the social systems involved, than with the processes which occur in the development.

These processes can be illustrated by assuming that it is an individual social worker that initiates the carers' support group referred to above. The motivation may have come from her own case experience, and an awareness of other such cases in the team; an awareness from reading in social work journals; and a personal interest in doing some group work.

This may seem to contradict the idea of the team approach which we argue is essential for community social work, but effective team work facilitates the individuality of members within a shared strategy, value, and task framework. Consequently it would be perfectly appropriate for an individual to initiate in this way. What is crucial is *how* she and the team manage the process of her initiative. Managed well, a possible action plan for creating a carers' group may include the following:

1. Because of uncertainty about her senior's and her team's view of the priority which should be given to this work, the social worker first discusses her idea, and strategies for pursuing it, with a friend in another team. Some possibilities emerge:

a) gather information from team clerks and domiciliary services about numbers of carers, and some illustrative cases of carers under stress who might use a support group. Go to senior and team armed with this data and proposal.

b) share the idea informally with senior, focusing on the worker's case and professional development needs in relation to group work, in order to assess and engage the senior's interest before sharing the information gathered and set out in (a).

c) contact a district nurse known to the social worker who participates in the community forum, who can raise the idea in that forum, at which the team senior will be present.

d) raise the general issue of work with elderly at a team policy meeting. Identify carers' group as one possible innovation for the team to consider in its transition to community social work.

There are many other possibilities. However, the main point is that *how* she goes about engaging others in the development of her proposal will affect the outcome crucially.

These processes can, to a degree, be considered and planned in a sequential way in the light of the worker's knowledge, values, assumptions and so on. How detailed this is, and how explicit, depends on the worker and her situation. In a sense, it can never be too detailed. The complexity is such that it will be easy to leave out something which later inhibits or blocks the innovation. Failing to notice, for example, that the department is funding a self-help group's project across the whole city, of which an aspect could be several carers' groups, may mean at a later stage that the social worker'a own area head will veto this particular scheme. That may be appropriate, but equally it may not. On the one hand, there are always too many factors to take into account, but, on the other, the effort still has to be made to make sense of them all in ways which facilitate the most effective and efficient ordering of steps in the process of innovation. 'Theory' is crucial here, since the theories we hold about the nature of organisation, group process, interpersonal influence and so on help us order this potentially boundless complexity.

2. Having shared the idea with a friend, the social worker may opt for next sharing the broad idea, and its basis, with her senior, who recommends bringing it to the team with some background data, and a written statement of aims and issues the team may have to consider.

Putting aside the question of whether or not the social worker *should* go along with her senior's strategy, she now has several routes depending on her particular context. Perhaps this social worker is relatively new to the team, and has previous experience of special projects. Because of this she may already be perceived by some colleagues as rather too challengingly innovative. The climate of the team may then be resistant to yet another 'good idea' from her, despite overt commitment to the generic changes implied by the shift to community social work, and despite overt validation of the principle behind the proposal for initiating the carers' group. Whether this matters will depend on the culture of the team.

3. The social worker may decide to include an intervening step by discussing her idea informally with a couple of team members, so that at least some people are prepared when it is raised more formally within a team meeting. How this is done, and with whom, also has to be considered. She may seek the involvement at this stage of the home help organiser and others from whom support can be expected, to back up her case before the full group.

For the initiative to get going, a complex network of 'permissions' may be required. These may be from managers higher in the hierarchy, but perhaps even more importantly, from immediate colleagues and people outside the organisation altogether. The theory of the organisation may suggest that senior management makes the crucial decisions. But in practice people in authority do not have a monopoly on the giving and withholding of crucial permissions. Such 'permissions' take several forms, not merely verbal assents to the idea. A colleague only really permits the social worker's engagement in the initiative if he engages in appropriate collateral activities, such as *actually* presenting the proposal with commitment to his clients; and *actually* allowing time for the project to be discussed in team meetings, etc. The social worker may have to continually 'service' such permissions to sustain the project over time in the context of a changing environment.

All the different possible steps which the social worker might have to go through sequentially have different time implications which have to be taken into account. It will always be tempting to short circuit some step or other, or, alternatively, to over-estimate the time needed for any particular step. How long will it *actually* take to arrange to meet the home help organiser and talk through the issues well enough to be able to present a convincing proposal to the team? This has all to do with acknowledging that developing a carers' group implies changes in a network of relationships for which the social worker has to take responsibility for understanding and facilitating, as thoroughly and skilfully as 'direct' work with clients.

4. After consultation and sharing within her team and her wider professional network, the social worker has identified a prima facie need; has read up on carers' groups and problems of the elderly; has spoken with various people from other statutory and voluntary agencies. As far as she can tell there are no insurmountable explicit or implicit obstacles to the project, and so she identifies the following specific factors which now have to be ordered into a sequence of actions:—

a) specify task and process aims of the project: "How will we know that the project has been successful?"

b) identify methods: "How are we going to do what and with whom?"

c) arrange supervision, consultancy and training for herself: "How do we get help, support and critical review of the work?"

d) identify time scales for setting-up; running; evaluating.

e) identify and negotiate for a location.

f) identify and arrange any transport needs.

g) identify and arrange any financial support.

h) identify and recruit group members.

i) work out monitoring and evaluation procedures.

j) identify and plan for workload implications for self and team.

5. How such variables are ordered into a sequence will be subject to many variables. All the elements will affect and be affected by all the others. They will have an impact upon the other process aims being pursued by the team, and in turn be influenced by them. Decisions over where to locate the group are involved with issues of aims, methods, transport, and finance. Perhaps the group ought initially to be convened in the team office so that then the group as a whole can work together on deciding whether a more favourable location is possible and needed. That approach may fit certain kinds of aims and assumptions more than others. If a carer wants to attend, but cannot leave a dependent relative, this would suggest a location where the relative could attend too. Or, alternatively, some extra 'sitting' service may need to be generated. Perhaps a local authority residential home could be used, as it could better cope with carers bringing their relatives with them? This would require negotiation and, perhaps, changes in expectation and practice from the officer-in-charge and her manager at County Hall. This will affect the time-scale, and shows how assessment and intervention are inseparable. In order to 'assess' the possibility of using the residential home to locate the group, it may be necessary to 'intervene', i.e. create a relationship with people which will facilitate rather than inhibit changes in expectation and behaviour. To obtain the resource may require changes in the relationships of the professional networks which constitute the resource.

This hypothetical linear action plan could be indefinitely extended. For example, all and any of the items listed in section 3 could themselves be the subject of step-by-step plans for action. Any and all of them will have connections with other process aims and their constitutive activities, which the social worker and her team may have to consider, and which will count as significant information to feed back into the process of change as a whole.

Stopping the story at this point is arbitrary in the same way as choosing a starting point on the paradigm spiral is arbitrary.

PART II

Ideas for a Practice Theory for Community Social Work: Synthesis or Compromise?

"It is quite wrong to try founding a theory on observable magnitudes alone. In reality the very opposite happens. It is the theory that determines what we can observe."
                    —EINSTEIN

Chapter 8

A Map of Community Social Work Activities

Introduction

A mixture of old and new ideas is often expressed in the way people respond to descriptions of community social work practice. They often fluctuate from "we do that already" to "that's impossible to do in our agency because . . .". The starting points of such descriptions of new practice may sound the same as those stated and propounded by more orthodox colleagues. But somehow those practising community social work have a knack of ending in a different place. In fact, the basic theory *is* different, even though it is understood intuitively by practitioners rather than articulated in the social work literature.

The first part of this book contains some basic assumptions, a description of a paradigm for change and illustrations of practice based on our own experience. Now we address the next stage of the paradigm: re-thinking our basic assumptions. We argue for a synthesis of ideas, a holistic view of social work practice to underpin social work activities and make sense of the social care planning *and* the counselling dimensions of community social work. In our view it is not enough for community social work to be a compromise, a collection of activities lumped together to suit the convenience of the day and the current trend in organisational philosophy.

We need a theory of human behaviour and human problems which explains why problems are sometimes resolved by our

111

interventions, while at other times the same problem presented in very much the same circumstances resists our efforts to bring about change. This does not mean our conventional approaches are entirely wrong, but that they are based on ideas that are significantly incomplete. What we are suggesting, therefore, is a synthesis of ideas based on a different starting point — not electicism.

Our starting point, made clear in Chapter 2, is the need to shift our thinking from focusing on identified clients to the relationships between people, from groups or 'classes' of people to the relationships between people across groups, classes and organisations. This shift in thinking from the parties in relationship to *the relationship* is deceptively easy to talk about, yet often extremely difficult to put into practice. In some ways it has even long been recognised. Most attempts to understand people and their problems refer to the influences of people on one another and the effect of other significant factors in the environment. Yet it is typical that one or other party in a relationship is held to be constant, or non-participatory. This never happens in real life.

What we need is a way of looking at people, social problems and their resolution which is both adequate in itself and also takes into account the fact that many of the standard theories and practices are right, yet insufficient.

The search for a synthesis: from competing activities to components of a whole enterprise

A new synthesis of ideas is necessary to avoid the old polarisations in the field of social care, of community work versus social case work; of voluntary help versus statutory services; of natural helping networks versus professional intervention; of social care planning versus counselling. Each phase in the history of social work has been characterised by similar debates, typically based on different starting points more than substantial clashes of evidence. (See Timms 1983.)

The opposition between working with 'the community' and working with 'the individual' is rooted in more fundamental and equally misleading divisions between psychology and sociology. Can we break out of this circle and allow social work to be shared with citizens? To do so we must shun these sterile polarised debates which contribute little or nothing that can benefit either social work's traditional customers, or the communities of which they are a part. Furthermore, they are an illusion of opposites. Watzlawick (1974) illustrates such illusions by telling the story of a resistance movement's activities in pre-war Nazi Germany. The National Socialists put up posters with the slogan "National Socialism or Communism?" The resistance movement added a sticker saying, "Spuds or Potatoes?"

The practice theory of community social work is still being forged. At present it is often a compromise, an eclectic view of social care. Like all eclectic views it is admirably liberal but, as in other fields of human activity, it is difficult to judge where liberalisation ends and promiscuity begins. If we are only concerned with the 'idea' of community social work, we can be all things to all people. But it is of crucial importance to practitioners to clarify the theory of community social work, if they are to make the right choices and be publicly accountable for their actions.

We are concerned here, therefore, with theory that relates to how you practice community social work. Next Monday, can you spend the morning counselling a client, developing his community cohesion, and politicising his neighbourhood, all at the same time? This, as we see it, reflects the crucial dilemma facing us over community social work. Unless we can begin to answer 'yes' to this question, then we lack an underlying theory for making sense of, and so integrating, social work activity. Social work agencies will continue to be constant prey to re-organisations which have little effect on what happens between social workers and other people.

The map of social work activities in Fig. IV attempts to illustrate the relationships between the different dimensions of community social work.

This map recognises that social work includes:—
— work with individuals and their immediate families and networks to tackle problems which directly affect them = DIRECT WORK

— work with wider community groups and other agencies to tackle problems which affect a range of people (including the individuals involved in direct work) = INDIRECT WORK

— work which involves the maintenance of certain social situations to avoid further distress or institutionalisation, by the provision of services = SERVICE DELIVERY

Fig. IV

MAP OF SOCIAL WORK AND SOCIAL SERVICES ACTIVITIES

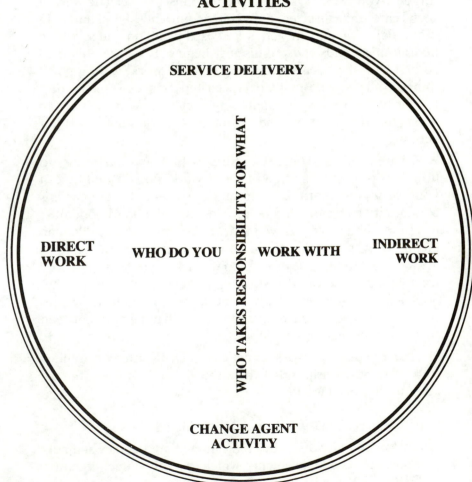

— work done to effect change in the ways people relate to each other, ways which precipitate or perpetuate social problems, whether in families, community groups or organisations. Workers intervene in agency/inter-agency practice, attempting to change procedures or how they are applied to particular people. Workers engage in community development activities as described in defining social care planning. Workers intervene with individuals and their immediate families to work with people to change their behaviour = CHANGE AGENT ACTIVITY.

Looking at this map, it is not difficult to see how any one referral could involve work in any of the four quadrants:—

A child care referral may start with direct counselling to the family designed to bring about change in family functioning: bottom left. If a day nursery place is provided to complement this work, a service is being delivered: top left. The existence of such a nursery — say, for example, run by the Children's Society — assumes that indirect work has been done. This work will be located in the top right quadrant if the social services department is funding. Bottom right would be the location of the work at the initial stages of such a project, especially if the social service department workers were working with resident groups to press an outside organisation to establish, or change the service provided.

There are several important issues to bear in mind when using this map to analyse social work and social services activity.

— To engage in change agent activity is to deliberately not take responsibility for the problem or its solution. Here the worker works with other people helping them bring about change.

— To deliver a service is to acknowledge and accept responsibility for a problem or its solution and so provide something to help solve that problem (often by maintaining the status quo or preventing further deterioration in a person's situation).

— The change agent/service delivery dimensions are typically blurred in many current discussions of social work. It is fashionable — and very unhelpful — to talk of all social service activity only in *service delivery* terms. We will discuss the place of social control in social work activity in Chapter 9.

— Changes in circumstances will move the location of work rapidly. For example, evidence of non-accidental injury will cause change agent work in family functioning to be supplemented by the service of alternative care for the child, or in further changes in the family and neighbourhood network.

— The diagram is only a *map,* not an axis along which things can be measured. It is a device for finding your way around. Features are abstracted, given symbols and plotted on the map to provide 'landmarks' for planning a journey or locating the opposition of one feature relative to another.

— The social work agency, and within it 'the team', has to address the *whole* of the task as represented by the map.

— Managers and teams managing whole tasks have to be aware of how work in one quadrant inevitably has consequences for work in the others. They also have to decide how best to allocate resources and divide labour, so that they maximise the impact on the whole task as described by the map. The question facing management is, "How do you organise a team or a department to have maximum impact on this whole task?"

The map takes us one step forward in the search for a bridging practice theory, by highlighting the inter-relationships between work at different levels and with different people. To go further, we need to discuss the nature of the social problems social work is designed to tackle.

Chapter 9

Social Work, Social Problems and Social Control

Social workers are employed because social problems exist within our society. A practice theory of social work should then start with an analysis of the nature of 'social problems', and face up to an issue often avoided in discussions of social work: the issue of social control. In doing this we will review the relationship between social problems and 'the community'.

Discussions of community social work often stress that there are untapped resources in communities and neighbourhoods which could be mobilised to support those in need. Critics of these approaches and of community care generally point out that all too often these views are based on the assumption that people, usually women, can be exploited to make up for deficiencies in existing networks of care. We do not advocate approaches to social care that perpetuate such exploitation. Indeed, it is fundamental to the argument presented here that change in patterns of care are essential for resolving many social problems. Critics have also drawn attention to the limitations of the kinds of care actually likely to be available in such networks. (See for example Equal Opportunities Council 1980; Finch and Groves 1983; Bulmer 1987; Sinclair et al 1988.)

Here we want to develop a different view.

The untapped resources in communities and networks are often talked of as if they were similar to reservoirs of oil under the seabed. All we have to do to develop these resources is to locate the oil and build a pipeline to areas of need, thus providing 'support'.

This way of looking at networks, communities, their needs and resources, overlooks the fact that these communities or networks can be said to *'cause'* all the problems social workers are called upon to resolve. 'The community' is not just a solution — 'the community' has created these problems in the first place. These resources — these potential network helpers — are currently busy doing other things. Formal helpers are working in the old ways; so are the semi-formal helpers, that is, organised volunteers. 'Potential helpers', be they next-door neighbours or relatives, are busy with their own lives, even if this just means being uncomfortably bored, aimlessly watching television. Most 'care' is being carried out by female relatives, assigned to the task by traditional assumptions, and held there by the threat of guilt and the absence of real alternatives. These people are left to cope as best they can. There is no evidence to suggest that there are queues of people sitting in a social vacuum waiting to help.

However, *it is impossible for a person not to be part of a community or network*. 'Community' (see Chapter 4) is a concept used to describe social relationships defined by geography, kinship or common interests. All people are part of social relationships which we, or they, might call a 'community'. A 'network' is a set of relationships between people. Taken in its widest sense, a person's network can mean all the contacts that person has, from the milkman he never sees to his closest relative. More specific networks can be identified, such as family or kinship, professional/work relationships and friends. Most people are members of different interlocking or overlapping networks. Given these definitions, it is impossible to imagine anybody who is not part of a network. Knowledge of such a person would be proof that somebody, somewhere, has some form of relationship with them.

The assumption that it is impossible not to be in a network is a corollary of the systems theory proposition that *all behaviour is communication*: to ignore, or to be totally unaware of one's next door neighbour is *to communicate* with him and to be *in relationship* with him. Although this relationship may have negative value, it cannot be described as 'no relationship at all'.

Many people are in networks which ignore, neglect, reject, persecute or in some other way cause them stress, or leave them alone with their pain. Most people are in communities and networks where resources are unevenly distributed, and some feel powerless relative to others. Often people known to social workers are in networks that label them 'clients'. The social worker will deliberately, or carelessly, but nevertheless inevitably, be part of these processes. Depending on how the social workers participate in these networks, they may confront or collude with the labels placed on people.

In some situations the social worker will accept, and be part of formulating, a definition of a problem that identifies a person or people as 'clients' of the department in need of the agency's services. Work will then proceed at the SERVICE DELIVERY end of the spectrum (see Fig. IV in Chapter 8).

The SERVICE DELIVERY dimensions of social work and social services are crucial to the quality of life of many and to the very survival of others. How services are to be delivered and what services should be on offer should continually change with the changing nature of social problems. Resources allocated to field social work staff, or residential care, for instance, may give way to domiciliary services as the balance of needs changes. We know of no evidence that suggests that community social work approaches reduce the overall level of resources needed for service provision. But a community social work approach should provide for greater flexibility of service provision, a wider range of resources and greater choice for consumers. Service providers also have more options on how they exercise their responsibility to meet people's needs.

However, there will also be many situations where the social workers will not, or cannot, take responsibility for the problem and its solution by providing such a service. Where workers reject the labels placed on people, are called upon to attempt to work with people to change their behaviour, or cannot provide a service, they must either turn the problem away or attempt to bring about change in the networks of which the people are a part. This CHANGE AGENT ACTIVITY is on the other end of the spectrum.

Social problems and the need for CHANGE

To say that people's needs should not be neglected is another way of saying that those people who could be meeting them should be behaving differently. It assumes that it should be possible for such people, be they neighbours, relatives, friends or staff in the personal social and health services, to behave in ways which enable unmet needs to be met. To make these implicit value statements explicit is to say that such people's behaviour deviates from norms that *should* apply. To neglect a neighbour is to deviate from the norm which implies or states that neighbours should help each other, albeit such deviance is very common, like speeding or petty dishonesty.

Increased levels of care cannot arise spontaneously — people identified as the community's 'resources' have to *change* if they are to meet the needs of others. Professional and informal carers will have to develop new forms of practice. Those in need of help are essential partners and will have to agree to receive it from new combinations of people if the pattern of care is to change. The people who currently control other, non-human, resources must also revise the part they play. What is required is a change in the attitudes, the expectations and sense of responsibility and, above all, the motivation of people to care for other people. A tall order maybe, but even that is only a part of what is needed to deliver the resources to where they are needed. The task almost makes the oil fields of the North Sea look like an easy place to go and work.

The elaboration of latent resources or 'growth' models of community development and social work seems to be embedded in a metaphorical view of human growth as development. This incremental evolution of theory (or is it compromise?) is insufficient because it fails to make a necessary conceptual shift, the move from developing the 'latent resources' of individuals and helping them to 'mature', to helping communities 'develop' and become responsible for the well-being of their members. In themselves these goals are difficult to criticise. But it is not a very helpful or an accurate enough way of looking at these issues. We take the view that all communities, like individuals, 'change' and continue to 'change'. We choose this as the appropriate term because it is more neutral than 'develop' and does not assume progress.

The recognition that people are inevitably part of networks and communities means we have to be explicit about the value judgments we make about these relationships. People create their communities and networks by the way they behave in their environment. These sets of relationships are as often 'dying' as they are 'developing'. They are in a constant state of transition, never static. As they change they throw up, create, that is, 'cause' and perpetuate the same problems that they are called upon to 'cure' or resolve.

To be more precise, we should say that these problems are features of the patterns of relationships we can observe or experience. 'Social problems' are *within* communities and networks; they are part of the fabric. Networks and communities are not outside them, to be applied as cures or supports. 'Problem' identification is a judgment by somebody in the network on the nature of some person or person's behaviour within a social system. Typically this is a judgment on a set of relationships. Intervention and theories of understanding what to do and how to do it should, then, focus on these relationships. To focus on one person or group of people per se is to miss the point. It is like listening to the notes without hearing the music.

Social networks, communities, social situations and the social problems within them only come about, like music, through the way component parts are put together over time.

The perception of 'the individual' as 'the cause' of social problems is often perpetuated by the way we conceive social problems. This is clearly demonstrated in Appendix A of the Barclay Report (1982), the patch advocates' minority report, a section where we might expect to find the greatest clarity about the relationship between social problems and community. They state:—

"We recognise that many areas and estates seem to have very little community spirit or identity". (p.220)

This is not so much an absence of solution but, as we see it, this *is* the problem.

"... we also realise that a community can be very hostile to individuals or groups within it, and that areas which seem to have the greatest social needs often seem to have the weakest informal networks. Our view of neighbourhoods is, in short, far from an easy or sentimental one." (p.220)

What are *social needs* if they are not in part a weak, informal network? Or, to put it another way, surely a weak informal network is seen as a social problem because needs go unmet.

They continue:—

"What we are emphasising is the fact that most dependent people whose needs come within the remit of the personal social services (the frail elderly, the mentally and physically ill, and the handicapped living in the community, families with children at risk, and others) are tied because of frailty, illness, fear, handicap, low income or habit to their local area, whether or not it has any sense of community." (p.220)

These quotes clearly illustrate the implicit assumption that problems come from within the individual, solutions from those around them or elsewhere. This is not 'untrue', but it is only part of the truth. It is too limited. A more complex, more systemic analysis will help us recognise the full complexity of the social worker's task as a change agent. A limited perception will also, incidentally, obscure how peripheral social workers normally are to the social lives of most people.

People have many problems, the causes located in many different aspects of their own attributes or their environment — in a strictly scientific sense the actual 'causes' are often not known.

A *social* problem is one where an initial problem or condition is not being met by the social circumstances of the client. Thus a frail, elderly woman unable to feed herself, fearful of being alone, and depressed about her physical condition, clearly has 'problems'. Some may say these 'problems' are an inevitable 'fact of life' and not a 'problem' at all, and call it 'ageing'. For her to be referred to a social work agency or in some other way to be seen as a '*social problem*' is more a comment on *how her problems are being met by others,* than on the condition itself. To focus on her and her needs alone is not only to ignore potential resources, it is to misunderstand the very nature of the *social problems* presented by this situation. When they do this, social workers stand little chance of producing positive change in the networks they have been called upon to help. They will depend on negotiating for state resources to help such people, and essentially take responsibility for these problems on to themselves as representatives of the state. This is a valid option and one which is vital for many people currently receiving social work help. But it is far from the only option, and when used routinely it compounds the social work tendency to 'clientise' all who ask or are referred for help.

We should recognise that SOCIAL PROBLEMS ARE THE MALFUNCTIONING OF A NETWORK OF PEOPLE. The network may be composed of family, friends or neighbours, or other members of a wider community. We know the vast majority of people's needs are met by carers in the community, without professional intervention. People's needs only become a 'social problem' when they are not met. Being old is not a serious problem any more than being a baby is one. Being either without having appropriate relationships with others is, however, a 'social problem'.

Service delivery and change agent interventions: a continuum of social work activity

Some people come to social work agencies asking for help. Others are involved by offering their help or through local associations or organisations, or through a relative, neighbour or friend's contact with a social worker. But many 'statutory' clients are *sent* because somebody else is concerned about their welfare or their behaviour. The doctor or health visitor suspects non-accidental injury or child neglect; neighbours call the police, or the courts refer a child for delinquency; a person's behaviour is seen as 'mad' by somebody, often a family member; a neighbour refers an isolated elderly person as in need of more care; relations refer an old person for residential care, and so on. These people are referred to social work agencies by other people in their social network. The pattern of behaviour determining such referrals is to cope with problems by extending the network to include social workers or other agency staff. Most people in the network will then attempt to delegate responsibility for the problem to the social work agency staff (non-accidental injury scandals make these processes plain and enquiries typically approve of such delegation).

It is crucial that social workers do not simply accept this delegation or responsibility. There are times when responsibility should be taken and when a service should be provided. Providing day nursery places, receiving children at risk into care, providing residential homes for the elderly, organising long or short term domiciliary services, are all examples of the kinds of services that might be provided. The local authority and other agencies' resources are used here to help maintain people 'in the community', to meet their needs by becoming an essential part of their network.

However, there are serious dangers in framing all social work activity as 'service delivery'. It hides, or at best obscures, the essential change agent dimensions of the social work task. Social workers who use a non-change theory — a 'support' and 'meeting need' definition of their role, are always going to fall into the trap of *becoming and remaining an integral part* of the systems they enter. This is most clearly seen in the way social workers literally become the supporting part of networks, and then quite 'rightly' assess the situation as one they cannot leave. The need for change in patterns of behaviour in the 'client's' network are not identified. Alternatively they are unsuccessful in achieving this change and are left themselves to fill the gap between 'what does' and 'what should' happen. Without a theory of CHANGE, the *redundancy* of the social worker in social situations where their presence should be transitory can be overlooked as an essential GOAL.

To use 'social networks' or draw on 'community resources' to resolve social problems means that social workers have to resist the pressure to become a permanent 'caring' part of people's networks. It means *changing the pattern of referral and problem delegation*; the way people in the network behave when faced with a social problem. A typical change agent response would be to explore alternative definitions of 'the problem' to that presented by the referrer; for example by engaging a relative and other professionals in a discussion of how they are currently managing the problem of a frail elderly person rather than immediately accepting the referrer's proposed solution of residential care. The circle of those engaged in this way widens, as the worker draws on local knowledge to seek alternative ways of managing 'the problem'.

A redefinition of the role of the professional may be necessary to achieve this change. "We pay you to help us solve these problems ourselves" as opposed to "We pay you, the experts, to solve these problems", is a much trickier brief for social workers to follow, especially when most referrals are clearly not made in this spirit. How do these issues affect assumptions about who should have power and control over social care? It is naïve to assume that people with power and control opt to take responsibility too. The way people become clients suggests the very reverse. Those with power often see 'clients' as 'the problem', and so hold them responsible for a social problem which is the malfunctioning of a set of interpersonal relationships. The implication of this conceptualisation of social problems is that professional intervention can clearly be seen to involve CHANGE in these networks or communities. We can now add to our assumptions the following:—

CHANGE IN A SOCIAL NETWORK CAN BE BROUGHT ABOUT IN THREE WAYS:—

— BY ADDING THE SERVICES OF THE SOCIAL WORK AGENCY TO THAT NETWORK TO MEET NEEDS WHICH CANNOT BE MET BY OTHER PEOPLE IN THE NETWORK.

— BY PROFESSIONAL INTERVENTION GEARED TO CHANGING THE PATTERN OF RELATIONSHIP WITHIN A SOCIAL SITUATION.

— BY SOME COMBINATION OF THE TWO WHICH CHANGES OVER TIME AS PROBLEMS CHANGE.

To change *the pattern or relationship* in social situations is to change both the individual and the behaviour of others in the network or community. The choice of focus of intervention is a technical matter about *how* to intervene, not a judgment about *what* to change. It is this analysis which leads us to say that the polarity between community work and counselling is an illusion. The choice between methods of intervention should be based on their likely effectiveness in meeting the problems confronting the social work agency. They should not be based on an ideological commitment to a particular approach; even less should they be chosen to sustain the current identity of a group of workers.

Deviance and community social work

There are times when it is cumbersome and pedantic to keep asserting that people are social animals whose behaviour can only be understood in the context of their relationships to others. However, this perception is crucial for intervention and change. Community social work will follow the 'unitary approach' and 'integrated methods' in giving us only a richer *description* of what social work should do unless the theory and practice implications of this view are taken seriously by social work organisations. Recognising the importance of understanding deviance and its implications is crucial to a change in practice.

DEVIANCE IS AT THE CORE OF SOCIAL WORK. Intervention is required because somebody defines a situation as one that *should not* continue as at present. Somebody says someone should care for this person — it is wrong that they are isolated or not cared for by relatives, neighbours or other people; a professional defines parents' behaviour as in need of change or so dangerous as to require removal of their children; or people want to change the quality of relationships between certain people or in a specified area.

People can become 'clients' because their needs are unmet by the networks they are part of. They can, of course, become clients because part or all of their network defines their behaviour as bad, mad, dangerous or difficult and calls upon someone else to do 'something about it'. The distinction, if it really exists at all, is between working with somebody who is a victim of others not putting desired values into practice — the isolated elderly person for example; and working with someone whose behaviour is defined by others as deviant — convicted offenders, for example.

The stress on deviant behaviour in precipitating or perpetuating social problems helps clarify understanding of the resistances to and complexities of effecting change.

This is the scale of the social work task, and why people are right to constantly raise the issue of values — they are clearly central. Debate must clarify and make explicit the social control issues that are such an integral part of *all* social work activities.

Social work is about trying to change patterns of interaction which perpetuate behaviour seen as 'deviant'. This may take the form of re-distributing resources so that people with unmet needs get more of those resources. Alternatively social work promotes 'conformity' to norms that are in some cases the law of the land, in others norms many people would like to see operating. They can be about violence to children, theft, drug-taking, bizarre and dangerous behaviour, or about the way we look after children or care for people with particular needs, or who are members of certain minority groups, or about the opportunities that people have to share in the well-being enjoyed by the majority of citizens and denied to some by the way some social and economic relationships operate.

No one occupational group or profession or organisation should have, or is likely ever to be given, power to define what we, citizens of this country, mean by deviant. Such definitions as there are, are typically the product of a range of negotiations, understandings, debates and political processes. SOCIAL WORKERS SHOULD ACTIVELY ENGAGE WITH A WIDE RANGE OF PEOPLE TO DEFINE THEIR GOALS AND OBJECTIVES AND SHOULD BE ACCOUNTABLE TO THE PEOPLE THEY SERVE. There is sufficient justification for this in the central place that deviance has in social work.

The 'power' of social workers

The power that social workers have and the authority they exercise is often a cause of concern. They are often seen as having 'too much power' over the lives of their clients. The need for social workers to limit their influence in the name of 'client self-determination' is an old, often debated area of social work education and philosophy. But a recent large-scale child care research review found that:—

> "There is an overwhelming impression of social workers' passivity and their feelings of helplessness and being at the mercy of events and actions of other people and agencies."
> (DHSS 1985, p.21)

So, are social workers very powerful or are they actually helpless? To answer this question would take another book. Here we will comment briefly on our understanding of power to make sense of both the 'powerful' and 'powerless' perception of social workers. This apparent contradiction results from confused perceptions about the nature of 'power'.

An interpersonal view of social relationships helps us recognise the reciprocal nature of power in social situations. The relationships which create or sustain 'deviant' behaviour are not based on the power of one individual or group, nor can the problem be solved by exercising 'power'. Relationships are based on a web of implicit and sometimes explicit agreements, collusions and individual decisions. To 'empower' people in these situations, it may be enough to help them recognise how they knowingly perpetuate circumstances which they could change, that is, to change their perceptions.

Perceptions play a dominant role in human affairs; their persistence is one reason why problems are perpetuated by patterns of relationships. The effective practice of social care and the management of change depends not on power exercised by a few but on partnership, between agents of the state and the whole range of citizens who are involved. Social workers need to make these partnerships productive, not by 'choosing' to share some of their power with clients, but out of recognition that many aspects of control over behaviour are beyond their grasp. Planned change requires working *with* people.

Direct and indirect work

Greenfly in the garden can be tackled with a garden spray. On a commercial scale this may cost much in resources. But such interventions can cause their own problems. If the insecticide used kills the ladybirds which eat the greenfly, then even more insecticide will be needed to kill the next crop of greenfly. Our understanding of ecology, and specifically the inter-relationships between different species, and their place in the environment, has changed the way we intervene in these problems. We can tackle such problems on an individual, or community wide basis. We can take more sophisticated action by inventing new insecticides which do not have harmful unintended consequences. We can change the balance of relationships between parts of the ecological system within which the problem occurs; we might now introduce ladybirds rather than use insecticides at all. Much time and money has been spent on understanding and developing solutions to such problems, more than is spent on research and development in understanding social problems and social work. Using an ecological model requires an understanding of the detailed way in which parts of the whole relate to each other; the same necessarily applies to community social work.

Direct service refers to work with individuals and their immediate families and networks, to tackle problems which directly affect them. Indirect work focuses on wider groups or classes of people — for example community groups and other agencies — to tackle problems affecting a range of people, some of whom may also be the subject of direct work.

Direct work with individuals or families identified as 'clients' is fairly self-explanatory and has probably dominated the focus of much orthodox social work. Indirect work involves the social care planning dimensions of social work and often has a preventative aim. This is widely considered to be a relatively neglected area in many social work agencies. (See, for example, Barclay Report 1982.)

Community social work involves intervening in networks or communities at different levels. It is necessary, though not sufficient, to continue to respond at the level of the needs expressed by individual families, or individuals and their immediate networks. It is equally necessary, but also not sufficient, to respond at the level of the wider networks of these families or individuals. These networks are often generalised as forming 'the context' of the family or individual. Helping a family with a crisis precipitated by bereavement or disablement may well require the direct intervention of a skilled worker. But taking on certain aspects of long term support after the crisis is over may not only be wasteful of professional resources but positively harmful. No further progress can be made unless links with other resources are established by successful work with wider networks with the space to care: networks which, to the identified family, may be seen as being at a contextual level.

Making a service available to a few, 'the most needy', may save resources in the short term, but only at the expense of those who receive those services and, in the long run, those who pay. To qualify people must satisfy certain criteria, or to put it another way, justify the label. Receiving the service then confirms that label. Such an approach perpetuates stigmatisation, and the web of reciprocal behaviour involved may then hold such people in their situations more firmly than straightforward material dependency upon the service (Smale 1984). Selective services concentrated on 'the most needy' also fail to prevent those not yet in the category from arriving at that point. Such people are often caught in a spiral of escalating unmet needs as their problems compound and exacerbate each other, since help is withheld until their situation is bad enough to demand it.

The cost of services to 'the most needy' is typically extremely high since they are, by definition, beyond the point where relatively small amounts can be spent, in either time or material resources, to maintain a potentially deteriorating position. In these ways direct service to the few often causes more resources to be spent on the few than might have been spent more effectively on indirect, preventative strategies targeted on a wider group of people.

Social workers as gatekeepers to resources: to keep the gate shut or to open it?

Throughout this book we have referred to the range of relationships and processes workers will engage in to carry out indirect work, both on behalf of existing 'clients' and to prevent problems with others. Here we want to make clear some of the more political dimensions of the social work task, the role social workers should take in social policy.

To be the gatekeeper to resources is to have power over those who want access to them, inasmuch as they want those resources and perceive the gatekeeper as controlling access.

This places an onerous responsibility on social workers to be fair, thorough and professional. They should also be clear about the finite limits placed on this power by the very real limits placed on their control of the allocation of these resources. Most local authority social workers' power over resources is actually very limited indeed, and social workers do themselves and their clients no favour by pretending that it is more or less than it actually is.

Social workers are constantly faced with the consequences of scarcity of resources, since many people's social problems are inextricably tied up with resource deprivation, such as lack of appropriate housing, employment, or insufficient income to meet needs. This is true by most objective criteria, let alone the subjective experience of the people involved. It is also the case that many people in a predominantly materialistic culture will define the solutions to a wide range of problems, be their origins personal, emotional or interpersonal, in terms of the acquisition of some new or different material resource. Problems with neighbours are presented as requests for re-housing, problems with children as requests for some extra facility, and so on. This compounds the demands on scarce public resources to supply jobs, housing and child care facilities, day and domiciliary services for community care, and so on.

An essential part of the social work task is the monitoring and communication of the extent and impact of these unmet needs. It is not enough merely to be frustrated by such deprivations as limiting the impact of a so-called professional service. The communication of these needs to policy makers is part of the task; an essential part of the professional role is to be active in constantly demonstrating the impact of deprivation on those it affects most. This will not make the image or role of the social worker any more popular or welcome. Social workers are not the first bringers of bad news to receive misplaced blame. But the political decision to re-allocate resources beyond the individual level does not lie with the social worker. Agencies and the professions as organised bodies need to raise their voices. The medical profession has a responsibility to make clear the health hazards of environmental conditions such as bad drains, and of diseases like AIDS. Social workers need to present policy makers with the evidence they collect of the social, psychological and emotional consequences of deprivation on the people they work with.

Yet even this is not enough. Although doctors are not expected to build drains or force local politicians to spend money on their construction, as a body they are expected to know how public health issues can and should be tackled. So it is with social work. Being employed as a social worker does not give a licence to become a full time political activist. Information and evidence should be passed to others whose job it is to bring about political change. We should be expected to draw on our expertise to offer guidance about the resolution of social problems, expertise gained through knowledge of the typical patterns of relationship between people, groups and organisations that precipitate or perpetuate the problems that recurringly plague our social lives. We do not claim that social work as a profession is yet fully equipped to fulfil this role. But it is nevertheless an important legitimate goal for social work to strive to make this contribution.

Within the local context, the social worker engaging in service delivery must necessarily act as an advocate on behalf of those she works with. But the role of 'change agent' is to empower other people, by providing information and helping them expand their abilities to present their case and achieve change. It is not the social worker's job to use these people and their problems to acquire a spurious moral base for her own power or to add authority to her own voice.

All too often direct and indirect work are presented as alternatives, rather than activities within the same situation at different but interrelated levels. Community social work is not work at one of these levels at the expense of another. It is a recognition that the individual can only change if there are changes within his social context: communities, neighbourhoods and networks can only change if the individuals within them change the way they relate to each other, and so change their behaviour as individuals.

At all levels, social workers are intervening in patterns of interaction so that the attitudes and behaviour of people change for the benefit of other people, and so that services may be delivered in the most effective way. More than this, they need to recognise that by working at any one level they are, in fact, intervening at other levels.

Without a strategy where work at one level is consistent with work at another, there are manifold dangers that all those involved in social care will cancel out each other's efforts. This underlines the need for collaborative working within the agency, and inter-professional, inter-department, inter-agency working between members of the agency and others. This is one facet of partnership: the resolution of unintentionally competing forces acting against good social care and problem-solving.

The location of work on the Direct-Indirect spectrum should be based on a judgment about what is the most effective way of tackling specific social problems, and what interventions can, and cannot, be avoided. Monitoring and evaluating the consequences of service delivery or change agent interventions is then fundamental. It is necessary to be clear about when direct intervention is essential; for example, in some child care or mental health emergencies. But all social work agencies have to avoid simply responding to the loudest voice demanding resources — the 'squeaky wheel gets the most grease' syndrome. Social care planning involves a thorough review of needs and resources, and consultations with a wide spectrum of consumers of social work and social service activity.

MARGINALITY: A note about the role of the social worker as change agent

Social workers know only too well that they are not employed simply to meet the needs of their 'identified clients'. They know that their job constantly involves balancing the expectations and demands placed upon them by different people: parents, children, health care professionals, teachers, the police, the magistrates, neighbours, senior managers, local politicians. These people may all expect the worker to respond in different ways to the same set of circumstances. Only an independent enquiry, working with the benefit of hindsight can be clear about what should have happened at crucial stages in case management.

Social workers who fail to hear what their clients say can never be good helpers and will rarely produce positive change in people's circumstances. Workers who hear, then immediately act to satisfy the demands of individual clients, fail to carry out the balancing act that is such an integral part of professional social work, and so fail to be part of the whole task of social work as illustrated by the Map (Fig. IV, Chapter 8).

What, then, is the role of the social worker and, specifically, her relationship with the networks that she works with? One of the difficulties for social workers is that they get sucked into the situation they are working with. Instead of entering a social situation to organise a service or attempt to effect change and then leave when the job is completed, the social worker becomes an in-built part of the network, often providing 'essential support'. This should occur in only a small minority of situations where special circumstances make any other alternative undesirable or most unlikely.

Social workers, however, must possess the ability to join with the people they are working with, if their help is to be accepted and if they themselves, or the services they provide, are to be seen as a legitimate resource. But essentially, the social worker is always 'marginal' to the networks she works with — joining but never becoming fully part of that network on a permanent basis.

The role of the social worker can be likened to that of a 'broker'. For example, the Barclay Report (1982) points out that this is often their role between employing authority and clients (para 7.28, p.111). This marginal role should be clear especially in situations of explicit deviancy, where the social worker has to understand both the deviant and those who stand for the status quo, both the delinquent and the magistrates. This marginality is essential for carrying out the task of effecting change in both, so that reconciliation can be achieved.

Being in a marginal position is a major cause of stress for social workers, just as for first line managers who are in an equally marginal situation, caught between senior managers and workers. Stress should be managed by appropriate staff support and development within the agency, not by attempts to reduce the worker's marginality in those social situations where the work to be achieved depends on that very marginality. Social workers are called upon to represent both their agencies, the wider community, and their 'clientele'. These needs are often in conflict, in work at all levels. For example, in the family: whose needs should the worker meet, the mother's or the child's? At neighbourhood level: the clash between "disruptive" families and "respectable" neighbouring families. And within the widest definition of community: the clash between the taxpayer's 'needs' and those of the 'needy'.

The marginal status of social workers pertains not just to their roles as brokers, negotiators and advocates, but also to their task in relation to social networks. TO UNDERSTAND AND PROMOTE CHANGE IN THE PATTERNS OF RELATIONSHIP IN SOCIAL NETWORKS, PRACTITIONERS NEED TO BE AT A 'META' LEVEL TO SUCH NETWORKS. To quote Bateson (1973), "You can't hear the music if you are one of the notes." This, like so many of the premises outlined above, has considerable implications for the training and management of practitioners. Sustaining a marginal role, constantly attempting to think 'outside' of the social situations while acting within them, requires awareness and skill not typically given much attention in social work training or staff development programmes.

Chapter 10

An Interpersonal View of Social Situations: Towards an Understanding of Change

"What element is it in human affairs that makes impossible, here, the exact mathematical prediction that is so brilliantly successful in our calculations about non-human nature? Evidently our unknown quantity in the realm of human affairs is a human being's apparent power of making choices."
— *Arnold J. Toynbee*

We define social intervention as attempts to resolve social problems, that is, 'deviant' or inadequate functioning of a social network. This definition is based on interactionist and systems theories of social relations. We call our view 'interpersonal' to stress our view of people as 'whole people', and not just components in social interactions. People are influenced by their environments, particularly their interpersonal relationships. But they do have some degree of choice; they can and do make choices about their behaviour, their relationships, and how they tackle problems.

Professor Parsloe has stated in an article on the training implications of the Barclay Report that:—

> "Social work education has, I think, been moving, albeit slowly, towards a more interactive view of human relationships and behaviour. The espousal of systems theory has provided an intellectual framework within which to site interaction. But neither interaction nor systems theory provide a sufficient base for community social work since that ultimately rests upon a value base."

Here we want to tackle what it means to take "a more inter-active view of human relationships". Systems thinking has influenced social work training, and books such as Pincus and Minahan's (1973) have become obligatory reading for social work students. However, it is by no means clear that it has really changed thinking and even less clear that it has affected practice.

Systems thinking takes us beyond many psychological or sociological theories, but often still not far enough. It is not enough for the social worker merely to recognise that people exist in two dimensional relationships with each other. The worker himself, when he intervenes, constitutes a third dimension: there is at least a triangle, between two or more 'participants' and the worker.

A practice theory based on a deliberately two dimensional view of social interactions is inadequate. Workers will always be in a three dimensional situation: they cannot minimise let alone eradicate the impact of their intervention. Indeed, as change agents, their role is to maximise their impact on social situations.

For the practitioner looking at the interactions of others, there can be no neutrality or absolute objectivity. 'Observing', 'assessing', 'getting to know' people and how they 'relate to each other', finding out 'what is going on' can only be achieved by intervening, by 'being there' and forming relationships with at least some of the other actors in the network under review.

Practitioners gather information through interaction, not by collecting 'facts' in an objective sense through responses to 'neutral' questions. What people say to a social worker about what they perceive as a social problem will reveal different things to different workers, depending upon their changing perception of their problem and their response to the behaviour of the worker, specifically how the worker in turn responds in the chain of responses that we call *interaction*.

Through such processes of intervention, feedback, hypothesising, a version of reality is negotiated by all those involved in the interaction (in practice, more than one version, since all parties to the interaction are engaging in the process). Our intervention perpetuates or changes the unfolding pattern of events. These processes cannot be neutral, objective, disinter-

138

ested, as if they were part of some 'scientific' procedure for defining a 'real' reality. Indeed, it is an essential assumption of interpersonal theory that no such 'reality' exists. PRACTITIONERS NEED TO RECOGNISE THAT THEY ARE WORKING IN A SEA OF DIFFERENT DEFINITIONS AND PERCEPTIONS OF 'THE REALITY' OF SOCIAL SITUATIONS.

Social workers need to develop expertise in understanding how different people define reality, and in working with these different definitions. People's experience, race, ethnic group, gender, class, religion all contribute to and are part of their view of the world. How they see themselves, the 'rightness' of relationships and what they define as a problem are all determined by these frameworks. It is not the social worker's job to 'define reality'. A central task is to develop mutual understanding, particularly when the need for change is disputed.

From this basis we can derive three further assumptions:—

THE FORMULATION OF A PROBLEM IS ALWAYS A JOINT ENTERPRISE BETWEEN WORKERS AND OTHER PEOPLE.

Workers cannot avoid being 'in partnership' with a range of other people in their work, but it seems to be the case that often many 'partners' are not treated as 'full partners', but as 'subjects' or 'objects' or 'clients'. 'Partnership' should mean that social workers forge explicit, open, equal and fruitful relationships to replace the status quo.

WORKERS MUST INCLUDE THEMSELVES AND THEIR INTERVENTION IN THE ASSESSMENT OF SITUATIONS, EXAMINING NOT ONLY HOW MEMBERS OF A NETWORK RESPOND TO EACH OTHER BUT ALSO HOW THEY RESPOND TO THE WORKER.

'ASSESSMENT', 'INTERVENTION' AND 'SERVICE DELIVERY' ARE ESSENTIALLY THE SAME ENTERPRISE.

Haley puts this succinctly, describing how the worker approaches his tasks. He is discussing 'why people change' in family therapy, but what he says has wider implications for those engaged in community social work:—

> "When one unit is more than one person, the cause of change must include more than one person. Typically, the family therapist talks to family members about understanding each other because they expect this, but he does not necessarily assume that this will cause them to change. He tends to see the change occur because of the ways he has introduced himself into a person's intimate network. How he sides with different family members, how he encourages or requires them to deal differently with each other, and how he shifts the responsibility for change back upon the family is considered central to change. Essentially the family therapist is introducing complexity into a narrow and rigid system." (Haley 1971, p.283.)

It should be noted that the therapist's role as described above, like that of the social worker acting as change agent, is essentially marginal: "he shifts the responsibility for change back upon the family".

Social interactions depend upon circular causation*

Ultimately, the strategy of producing change through social interaction presupposes a particular view of causality. The analysis of individual or collective behaviour often presumes a linear chain of cause and effect. We talk of events shaping the person or community as if they were pieces of wood, but in doing so ignore the essential inter-relationships between people. We overlook the fact that people act as well as respond, and that others respond to these actions, provoking further response, and so on.

In extracting the individual from his social milieu we do more than cut down on the variables. Typically, 'time' is also frozen; the person becomes an 'object', consisting of components made up of different historical or social influences. By implication some of the human aspects of this 'object' are overlooked. We remind ourselves that he or she is subject to a 'life-cycle', but, all too often, this is reduced to a series of snapshots — birth, childhood, adolescence, young adulthood, maturity, retirement,

* These concepts are based on the work of Watzlawick and his colleagues. (Watzlawick, Weakland and Fisch 1974.)

140

old age, death. The decision-making, pro-active, thoroughly human dimensions of this 'object' are obscured. We forget 'that person' is like us in all respects, even in terms of 'self-determination'. But, before we get lost in the tangles of 'choice' and 'freedom', how are we to make sense of the never ending spirals of this circular causality?

Usually one person or group of people are held responsible for what goes on, particularly what goes wrong, in relationships or social situations; that is, SOCIAL EVENTS ARE PUNCTUATED: THE STREAM OF EVENTS IN SOCIAL RELATIONSHIPS ARE TYPICALLY MARKED OUT, OR DIVIDED INTO A STRING OF CAUSE/EFFECT RELATIONSHIPS.

This process is illustrated by Watzlawick as follows:—

". . . probably as old as studies of this kind (stimulus — response experiments in psychology) is the joke about the laboratory rat who boasts to another, 'I have trained my experimenter so that every time I press the lever he gives me a piece of cheese.' What this rat does is simply to impose a different punctuation on the stream of events: what, to the experimenter, is the rat's response, the rat considers its stimulus to the experimenter; what he then does and calls a reinforcement, the rat sees as a response, and so forth." (Watzlawick and Beavin 1977, p.64.)

In human affairs such disputes over punctuation are far more serious and far-reaching. Were the Brixton, Toxteth and Tottenham riots *caused* by 'police provocation' or 'the behaviour of delinquent youths', or by 'those youths' families', or by 'unemployed people', or by 'racial discrimination' or 'poor housing', or by . . .? The answer is 'yes' in each case. We need a theory which can cope with such complex perceptions, by focusing on reciprocal interactions between actors and not simply on the actors themselves; by recognising that effects are often causes which are then effects; and by looking beyond intrinsic factors to help us see the patterns which connect those factors.

The concept of 'punctuation' in social events enables us to recognise that the imposition of 'cause and effect' analyses on these situations is at best partial, both in the sense of being incomplete and also in the sense of being biased.

The Russians blame the Americans for the arms race, the Americans blame the Russians who blame the Americans. It may be the case that one party was at one time 'the cause' of the problem. But now that is only of historical relevance; it is the pattern of relationships that has to change. Both parties need to change in such situations. Tackling one, then the other to achieve such change is often ineffectual, the action of the second provoking the re-cycling of the pattern before work with the first can be completed.

It must therefore be acknowledged that DEVIANT BE-HAVIOUR, BEHAVIOURAL PROBLEMS AND OTHER BEHAVIOUR TYPICALLY PRESENTED FOR 'HELP', SUSTAINS THE CONCOMITANT BEHAVIOUR OF OTHERS WITHIN THE SAME SOCIAL NETWORK OR SYSTEM.

Since social problems involve more than one person, and 'problem' behaviours are in part a response to a particular situation, it necessarily follows that symptomatic behaviour is in some senses 'appropriate' behaviour. It dovetails with that of others and often has the consequence of maintaining the pattern of people's relationships. Within this context it makes sense, even when it looks irrational, 'mad' or 'bad' when taken out of context, or judged by external standards. The question that needs to be asked is: what sort of situation is perpetuating this kind of adaptation? The forces perpetuating the status quo may be experienced as resistances to change by those trying to help. (See Smale 1984 for examples and further discussion of such relationships.)

Even if problems are not demonstrably initiated or 'caused' by the interactions in people's immediate or extended network, they can be perpetuated by them.

It follows, therefore, that: A CHANGE IN AN INDIVI-DUAL'S BEHAVIOUR OR CIRCUMSTANCES WILL CAUSE CHANGE IN THE PATTERNS OF INTERACTION OF WHICH HE IS A PART.

This can be stated negatively to emphasise the natural resistance to such change: AN INDIVIDUAL'S BEHAVIOUR IN HIS RELATIONSHIPS WITH OTHERS CAN ONLY CHANGE TO THE EXTENT THAT OTHER PEOPLE IN THAT SYSTEM CHANGE THEIR RECIPROCAL BEHAVIOUR.

First and second-order change

Social situations are characterised by two different types of change, depending on which part of the system is affected: the people in social networks or organisations; or the system as a whole, the 'family', 'neighbourhood' 'agency', or 'network' made up of part family, part neighbourhood, part agency. We can illustrate this by looking at the example of a family where the parents are locked in a struggle. The mother might lose out and be dominated by her husband; the children might form an alliance with the mother and the father may begin to lose out to his wife. Things do change, for better or for worse, depending upon who you are and what is happening within the system. However, the family remains a 'family locked in struggle'. For this 'struggle' to be turned into, say, 'co-operation', another sort of change is required, not just a change within the pattern of relationships, but a change in the nature of the pattern itself.

Watzlawick and his colleagues use the mathematical theory of groups and the philosophical theory of logical types to analyse these basic differences. They summarise their analysis as follows:—

"Group theory gives us a framework for thinking about the kind of change that can occur within a system that itself stays invariant; the Theory of Logical Types is not concerned with what goes on inside a class, that is, between its members, but gives us a frame for considering the relationship between member and class and the peculiar metamorphosis which is in the nature of shifts from one logical level to the next higher. If we accept this basic distinction in more behavioral terms: a person having a nightmare can do many things *in* his dream — run, hide, fight, scream, jump off a cliff, etc., but no change from any one of these behaviors to another

143

would ever terminate the nightmare. *We shall henceforth refer to this kind of change as first-order change.* The one way *out of* a dream involves a change from dreaming to waking. Waking, obviously, is no longer a part of the dream, but a change to an altogether different state. *This kind of change will from now on be referred to as second-order change.* . . . Second-order change is thus *change of change.*" (Watzlawick et al 1974, pp.10, 11.)

To increase the numbers of people receiving a service of the agency, or to change some part of the service, would be a first-order change. To change the way the needs are met by organising a self-help or community-based group would be a second-order change. There is no simple relationship between first-order change and service delivery, second-order change and change agent activity. However, it is probably true to say that much service delivery does not intentionally change patterns of relationships within social networks. The person or people receiving the service are sustained by adding resources to the existing patterns of care. This can set up a chain of changes which does change the pattern of relationships; taking children into care would be such an exception, although such intervention can be described as both a service delivery activity for the child, and a change agent activity to the family.

Change agent activity is more often aimed at changing the nature of patterns of relationships. Examples include:—

— changing the scapegoating role of a delinquent adolescent within his family;

— changing a network of relationships so that an elderly person is regularly visited;

— changing referral procedures or the ways in which a primary health care team and social work team relate to each other and their shared clientele.

Second-order change is achieved by going outside of the field of interaction within which the problems presented are locked. It usually comes about through novel solutions, as compared to the 'normal' solutions that might be offered from within the assumptions held by members of an existing network. This is the essential value of 'outsiders' in attempts to change intransigent

144

social situations. It is not unusual for such 'solutions' to be fairly simple, even if they are fundamental and difficult to achieve.

Towards a new practice theory

Much of the theory remains to be developed, and we are acutely conscious that there are many things we do not know how to change. However, we can make three theoretical generalisations about the components of change in social relationships. To achieve change, workers need to:—

— REFRAME THE PROBLEM: Some problems are perpetuated by people being locked into obsolete perceptions of situations, or of people's behaviour, or of each other; or having a limited view of options and alternatives; or through a perception of themselves as powerless and unable to behave in any alternative way. Problems that are defined as insoluble clearly need to be redefined if change is to take place; workers need to confront existing perceptions of problems where these seem to maintain the status quo.

— DEMONSTRATE ALTERNATIVE BEHAVIOUR: Patterns of behaviour are often repeated through lack of behaviour options. 'New' behaviour often has to be demonstrated if the risks of change are to be faced and behaviour repertoires expanded.

— PROMOTE A RE-ALLOCATION OF RESOURCES: This may be through existing mechanisms of distribution, or involve a second-order change: a change in the patterns of resource allocation. Resources may be financial or human, in terms of the ways people use time with each other.

We opened Chapter 2 of this book with a metaphor about Christopher Columbus and the difference made whether the world is seen as flat, or recognised as round. We do not want to claim that any of the ideas in this book are as significant or important as this basic discovery. However the metaphor is useful. Seeing the individual as *having a problem,* or seeing social problems as a *feature of a set of interpersonal relationships* is a conceptual shift of the same kind. The metaphor can also carry us forward, and suggest ideas yet to be developed.

A new perspective

The earth is not the centre of the universe but one of the sun's satellites. Individuals, like the earth and the sun in its turn, are not the centres of their 'universe' but only centres of attention for specific purposes. To understand the relative 'positions' of the earth and the sun, and to a large degree their behaviour, we need to perceive a whole set of patterns of relationships within the solar system, between the solar system and other entities in the galaxy and beyond.

But the metaphor must not be carried too far. People in relationships are not like suns and planets, obeying the laws of nature and rotating in predictable orbits through fixed relationships to each other. In human systems, the speed of change is rapid by comparison, but more significantly, people have some possibility of choice, even it they do not always exercise it.

Rather it is as though the earth, sun, planets and stars were drawn to their orbits by physical forces, but then could decide whether to continue with, or struggle against, their 'natural' paths. When one planet or person leaves their path, the whole pattern of the system is disrupted; everything must change. The choices for other entities are at once restricted and liberated. The patterns of social life are more like those of ants' nests than models of the solar system, but even this is an over-simplification: for it looks as though people were constantly and rapidly choosing to change the order of the nest. We, the human race, are continually making choices which change the environment, which makes any kind of 'nest' the best fit for the species in the ecology of the area. To believe in 'patterns' when faced with such complexity is to assert that it is possible to make some sense of what is going on, and so leave open the possibility of change through planned intervention. To try to reduce the complexity for the sake of easy understanding does violence to one or other of the essential ingredients in the puzzle.

It would be simpler to look just at one entity, the individual, 'as if' everything else were equal, to hold time still and treat human systems as mechanistic rather than organic. Certainly it seems easier to treat people 'as if' they were subject to deter-

146

mining forces; such assumptions hold the promise of predictable outcomes to certain interventions. We could talk about giving them choice or self-determination, as if they were 'ours' to give.

The trouble with all these limited versions of maps of social systems is that people just are not like that. Interventions based on limited maps are doomed to the twin failures of unpredictable effectiveness and unintended consequences. Somehow we must learn to grapple with the infinite choices and causes that shape social situations. We need to be able to identify patterns, make value judgments about the desirability of these patterns, and continuously intervene to make changes, to monitor the expected and unexpected impact of interventions and other changes; that is, to identify new patterns, make value judgments about the desirability of these patterns, and so round the spiral again. It is much more than a job for life.

It is far more than a job for one profession or one type of agency. Social work has its niche in these patterns, and will find particular relevance in those interactions that revolve around social care. Here social workers and other social service workers should struggle to achieve effective patterns of care and social control around the issues which they endeavour to change. The particular nature of this endeavour places a responsibility on them to struggle for an awareness of how patterns in our social relationships work, disadvantaging particular people and perpetuating undesirable behaviour. It also places a responsibility on them to be fully accountable to the people they work with and the people they work for. In so doing, social workers will play a part, marginal yet crucial, in the social care relationships within our society and work with, and against, others to make social systems 'better'.

References

Abrams, P. (1980) 'Social change, social networks and neighbourhood care'. *Social Work Service*. February, No. 22, pp. 12-23.

Barclay Report (1982). *Social Workers: Their role and tasks*. (London: Bedford Square Press).

Bateson, G. (1973) *Steps to an Ecology of Mind*. (St. Albans: Paladin).

Bayley, M., Seyd, R., and Tennant, A. (1985) *Neighbourhood Services Project — Dinnington Paper No. 12: The Final Report*. (Sheffield: University of Sheffield).

Beecher, W. (1987) *Directory of Community Social Work Initiatives: Scotland*. Compiled by W. Beecher for the Scottish Network for Community Social Work. (London: NISW: PADE).

Bennett, B. (1980) 'The sub-office: A team approach to local authority field work practice', in M. Brake and R. Bailey (eds.), *Radical Social Work and Practice*. (London: Arnold).

Bennis, W. G., Benn, R., Chin, R., Corey, K. E. (1976) *The Planning of Change*. (New York: Holt, Rinehart and Winston).

Beresford, P., and Croft, S. (1986) *Whose Welfare? — private care or public services*. (Brighton: Lewis Cohen Centre for Urban Studies at Brighton Polytechnic).

Bulmer, M. (1987) *Social Basis of Community Care*. (London: George Allen and Unwin).

Cooper, M. (1980) 'Normanton: Interweaving social work and the community'. In R. Hadley and M. McGrath (1980) *op. cit.*

Crosbie, D., Smale, G., and Waterson, J. (1987) *Monitoring and Appraisal of Scottish Network Development Group*. (Report to Scottish Office). (London: National Institute for Social Work, Research Unit).

Currie, R., and Parrott, B. (1981) *A Unitary Approach to Social Work — Application in Practice*. (Birmingham: British Association of Social Work).

DHSS (1985) *Social Work Decisions in Child Care: recent research findings and their implications*. (London: HMSO).

Egan, G. (1986) *The Skilled Helper*. Third edition. (Monterey, California: Brooks Cole).

Equal Opportunities Commission (1980) *Caring for the Elderly and Handicapped: Community Care Policies and Women's Lives*. (Manchester: Equal Opportunities Commission).

Finch, J., and Groves, D. (eds.) (1983) *A Labour of Love: Women, Work and Care*. (London: Routledge and Kegan Paul).

Goldberg, E. M., Gibbons, J., and Sinclair, I. A. C. (1985) *Problems, Tasks and Outcomes — the evaluation of task centred casework in three settings*. (London: George Allen and Unwin).

Hadley, R., and McGrath, M. (eds.) (1980) *Going Local: Neighbourhood Social Services*. NCVO Occasional Paper One. (London: Bedford Square Press).

Hadley, R., Dale, P., and Sills, P. (1984) *Decentralising Social Services: a model for change*. (London: Bedford Square Press).

Hadley, R., and McGrath, M. (1984) *When Social Services Are Local — the Normanton experience*. (London: George Allen and Unwin).

Haley, J. (1971) 'Family therapy: a radical change'. In: Haley, J. (ed.) (1971) *Changing Families*. (New York: Grune and Stratton).

Hearn, B., and Thomson, B. (1987) *Developing Community Social Work in Teams: A Manual for Practice*. (London: NISW: PADE).

Hedley, R. (1985) *Measuring success — a guide to evaluation for voluntary and community groups*. (London: Advance).

Henderson, P., and Scott, T. (1984) *Learning More about Community Social Work*. (London: National Institute for Social Work).

Henderson, P., and Thomas, D. (1985) 'Out into the community'. *Community Care*, 1.8.85, pp.17-19.

Henderson, P., and Thomas, D. N. (1987) *Skills in Neighbourhood Work*. Second edition. (London: George Allen and Unwin).

Holder, D., and Wardle, M. (1981) *Teamwork and the Development of a Unitary Approach* (London: Routledge and Kegan Paul).

Honor Oak Team . *Great Oaks from Little Acorns Grow: Reports of the Honor Oak Team 1978-80 and 1980-81*. (London: Lewisham Social Services Department, Honor Oak Sub-office).

Marris, P. (1974) *Loss and Change*. (London: Routledge and Kegan Paul).

Miller, C., and Scott, T. (1984) *Strategies and Tactics: Planning and Decision Making in Social Services Fieldwork Teams*. NISW Paper 18 (London: National Institute for Social Work).

Morgan-Jones, R., et al (1988) *Training Social Workers for Group Work*. (London: NISW: PADE).

Newcastle Social Services Department (1986) *Internal Report*.

Patti, R. (1983) *Social Welfare Administration: Managing social programmes in a development context*. (New York: Prentice Hall).

Payne, C., and Scott, T. (1982) *Developing Supervision of Teams in Field and Residential Social Work* (Part I). (London: National Institute for Social Work).

Pincus, A., and Minahan, A. (1973) *Social Work Practice: Model and Method*. (Itasca, Illinois: Peacock).

Pinker, R. (1982) 'Minority report' in Barclay Report (1982) *op. cit.*

Schon, D. (1983) *The Reflective Practitioner*. (London: Temple Smith).

Seyd, R., Tennant, A., Bayley, M., and Parker, P. (1984) *Neighbourhood Services Project — Dinnington Paper No. 8*. (Sheffield: University of Sheffield).

Sheldon, B. (1980) *Use of Contracts in Social Work* (Birmingham: British Association of Social Work).

Sinclair, I. A. C., Crosbie, D., O'Connor, P., Stanforth, L., and Vickery, A. (1988) *Bridging Two Worlds: social work, paid and unpaid care for elderly people living alone*. (Aldershot: Gower).

Smale, G. (1983) 'Can we afford not to develop social work practice?' *BJSW* Vol. 13, pp.251-264.

Smale, G. (1984) 'Self-fulfilling prophecies, self-defeating strategies and change'. *BSJW*, Vol. 14, pp.419-433.

Smale, G. (1987) 'Some principles of interactional skills training'. *Social Work Education*, Vol. 7, No. 1.

Smale, G., and Sinclair, I. A. C. (1988) *Evaluating Social Care: Management and Research Perspectives*. (London: National Institute for Social Work: PADE).

Stevenson, O., and Parsloe, P. (1978) *Social Services Teams: The Practitioner's View*. (London: HMSO).

Stocking, B. (1985) *Initiative and Inertia: Case Studies in the NHS*. (London: Nuffield Provincial Hospital Trust).

Timms, N. (1983) *Social Work and Social Values*. (London: Routledge and Kegan Paul).

Watzlawick, P., Weakland, J. H., and Fisch, R. (1974) *Change: Principles of Problem Formation and Resolution*. (New York: Norton).

Watzlawick, P., and Beavin, J. (1977) 'Some formal aspects of communication'. In Watzlawick, P., and Weakland, P. H. (eds.) *The Interactional View:* (New York: Norton).

Willmott, P. (with Thomas, D.) (1984) *Community in Social Policy* (Discussion Paper No. 9). (London: Policy Studies Institute).